The Catholic Family

The Catholic Family

THE EDUCATION OF CHILDREN

HOW TO RAISE HAPPY, HOLY CHILDREN IN A PROFOUNDLY CATHOLIC HOME

Volume II

FR. PATRICK TROADEC, SSPX

Translated by Mary Molliné

PO Box 217 | Saint Marys, KS 66536

Originally published as *La famille catholique* (Clovis).

Translated from the French by Mary Molliné.

Library of Congress Control Number: 2021901747

ANGELUS PRESS
PO Box 217
St. Marys, Kansas 66536-0217
Phone (816) 753-3150
FAX (816) 753-3557
Order Line 1-800-966-7337
www.angeluspress.org

ISBN: 978-1-949124-74-3
FIRST PRINTING–February 2021

Printed in the United States of America

Contents

BOOK TWO
THE EDUCATION OF CHILDREN

BOOK TWO

THE EDUCATION OF CHILDREN

Faced with a society that is changing quickly, faced with a Church in a state of crisis, many parents wonder: "What is going to become of our children? Will they be able to keep the moral and religious convictions we have sought to pass on to them?"

The examples of Catholic parents who were able to pass on to their children the best of what they had to offer are a beautiful encouragement for young families. It is good to see how they obtained these results.

The first step is to recognize the qualities and defects of a child after his Baptism. Based on this reality, we can define the nature and goal of education. Such will be the objective of our first chapter.

Given the claims of the Revolution, we shall then consider whose mission it is to educate in the first place. This will make it easy to understand the role of the parents.

Lastly, we shall consider the role of other educators in the chapters entitled, "Catholic School" and "The Art of Being Grandparents."

ARTICLE 1

Learning the Christian Life

CHAPTER ELEVEN

The Child: A Fallen and Ennobled Creature

In order to educate a child, it is necessary to know him, that is, to discern both his weak points and his strong points.

What is a child? He is a creature that is both weak and endowed with a great dignity. By his nature, he is a child of man and a sinner; but by the grace of Baptism, he is an adopted child of God and a "candidate for blessed eternity,"[1] which will crown his fidelity.

I – The Child at Birth

Man is a being of a spiritual nature, but he is neither a pure spirit nor a simple animal. He possesses faculties or abilities that the animals also possess (external senses, memory, imagination, *etc.*) and others that the angels also possess (intelligence and free will).

He must not take himself for an angel and neglect his body, nor must he lower himself to the rank of a simple animal and live according to his passions, following his instincts without thinking. Endowed with reason, he is capable, through his intelligence and his free will, of discerning the true, the beautiful, and the good, and of acting accordingly.

In order to refine this description, we have to be aware of the weaknesses left in Christians by original sin and of the resources with which Baptism enriches them. Indeed, ever since Adam's sin, man's faculties remain capable of attaining their object, but they now do so only with difficulty, even after Baptism, so long as the virtues are not acquired.

---

[1] Tertullian, *On the Resurrection of the Flesh*, Ch. 58.

Man, by his intelligence, is thus capable of discerning the truth, but he can be attracted by error. Indeed, he tends to be blinded by the goods of this world due to the wound of ignorance that afflicts his intelligence and to the disorder of his will and his sensitive appetites. He still remains capable of choosing the good, but when he is left to himself, he easily slides towards evil. It is difficult for him, therefore, to constantly keep the spiritual part of his being in control of the animal part, because of the wounded nature he has inherited from Adam and Eve.

Bishop Lecoeur told his faithful in a pastoral letter in 1931,

> Unless we are blind, we must, even in the best-behaved children, watch out for the awakening of certain inclinations explained by original sin. It is this mystery that enables us to understand man with his greatness and littleness; as Pascal says, man is more incomprehensible without this mystery than this mystery is incomprehensible to man.[2] An educator therefore has to act not upon an ideal, perfectly good child, but upon a real child, often so difficult to know because of the complexities and contradictions of his nature.[3]

2 – The Baptized Child

However, God fortunately enriches the child at his Baptism with a spiritual aide destined to correct his weaknesses and raise him up to the supernatural order. Indeed, man being called to share in the very happiness of God in Heaven, he receives here below a participation in God's own life. That is the teaching of the Church, transmitted by Bishop Pasquet to his faithful in 1927:

> Revelation teaches us that "by an effect of His exceeding charity" (Eph. 2:4), God wished to assign us a supernatural destiny and deigned to admit us to partake in His own life. Sin had taken it away from us; but Jesus Christ, by His death, merited for it to be restored to us; and it is this life that the Church henceforth dispenses to the child when he comes to request holy Baptism.
>
> From this moment on, divine grace dwells in him. A son of man by nature, he becomes through this mysterious rebirth a child of God, a brother of Jesus Christ, a member of the Church. His family is therefore no longer limited to the circle that witnessed his birth, nor his goods to the goods

---

[2] Blaise Pascal, *Pensées*, Gallimard, 2004, p. 115.

[3] Bishop Paul Lecoeur, bishop of Saint-Flour, *Lettre pastorale*, 1931.

> of the earth. As he now has God for Father, Heaven is his heritage. His obedience, here below, to the divine law, will allow him to earn it, and death, putting an end to the time of his trial, will enable him to possess it for all eternity.[4]

We might add that along with sanctifying grace, the child receives the infused theological and moral virtues and the gifts of the Holy Ghost to enable him to accomplish acts of a supernatural value, meritorious for eternal life.

Since the child has a supernatural destiny, parents will be very careful to make him live in a supernatural atmosphere. Bishop Mégnin declared forcefully:

> Your child is first and foremost a Christian. Rather, we might say he is only a Christian; no thought, no word, no act, no action, in any domain, must ever come from him, during his life here below, that is not animated by a Christian spirit, worthy of a child of God, and consequently able to strengthen daily the bond of love that unites him to the Blessed Trinity of which he is the temple, and to procure for him the eternal union of Heaven.[5]

---

[4] Bishop Octave Pasquet, bishop of Séez, *Lettre pastorale*, 1927.

[5] Bishop Jean-Baptiste Mégnin, bishop of Angoulême, *Lettre pastorale*, 1935.

CHAPTER TWELVE

Education, Its Nature and Goal

I – The Nature of Christian Education

Definition

Our hasty description of man with his fallen and renewed nature makes it easier to grasp the educator's mission and will now enable us to define it.

Etymologically, *education* is the art of *raising* a child. Raising a child means helping him to draw from himself that which is contained in him and to grow physically, intellectually, morally and spiritually in his entire natural and supernatural being.

The office of the educator, therefore, is to develop all the potentialities of the child, in view of the lofty destiny he has to fulfill. To do so, he needs to keep in mind both the weaknesses of the child and his good dispositions.

As the bishop of Saint-Flour said in the letter quoted above:

> Education includes two acts that, although theoretically distinct, must be accomplished simultaneously: bringing out all the child's qualities and correcting his defects; reform and progress, that is the double movement.
>
> We were just praising the charms of the child and saying that it is impossible to see him without loving him; but truth obliges us to admit that he is not an angel, though we sometimes affectionately call him one. He has at least the seeds of defective tendencies whose development must be prevented by a wise and prudent education.[6]

---

[6] Bishop Paul Lecoeur, bishop of Saint-Flour, *Lettre pastorale*, 1931.

While carefully correcting the child's defective tendencies, the educator will encourage the practice of virtue.

It is thus a matter, as Bishop Lecoeur says, of "working with God for the evolution of the natural and supernatural life of the child; that is the work of education."[7]

The Acquired Virtues

In order to give the best of himself, the child will have to acquire certain virtues: humility, obedience, purity, fortitude, *etc.*

Virtues are acquired by the repetition of acts. The human faculties, intelligence, will, and the appetites, are malleable at first, and determined by their own acts. By repeating the same acts, the child acquires an ability to accomplish them more easily and masterfully.

Virtue is a disposition so stable that the child is able to use it whenever he wants and with ease and pleasure. Man is made to live virtuously. It is the desire of his properly human nature.

St. Thomas Aquinas describes virtue as a good quality of the mind, by which we live righteously and of which no one can make bad use.[8] It is virtue that enables a man to possess himself. What is more, by perfecting the intelligence, the will, or the senses, the acquisition of a given virtue enriches man as a whole.

We therefore should not consider virtues as inclinations that go against man's well-being. While it is true that they oppose the disordered appeals of his fallen nature, they enrich his nature as a rational being. For example, humility is not contrary to man's nature in the sense that humility consists in remaining in the truth, to borrow St. Teresa of Avila's expression.[9]

The Infused Virtues

Besides the natural virtues he acquires by repeated practice, the child receives the seeds of the supernatural virtues at his Baptism. These virtues, both the moral and the theological virtues, will enable him to acquire supernatural merits when he reaches the age of reason.

Take faith, for example. Faith enlightens the intelligence and gives the child another perspective than that of simple reason concerning his

---

7 *Ibidem.*

8 *Summa Theologica*, Ia IIae, q. 55, a. 4.

9 St. Teresa of Avila, *The Interior Castle*, Sixth mansion, Ch. 10.

nature, God's nature and the means for reaching Him. It is developed by the teaching of supernatural truths, as Bishop Mégnin implied when he wrote:

> The baptized soul, this new member of the great Christian family, will not be led towards his supernatural destiny blindly and as it were by instinct. Indeed, he must know this destiny, and know this Father in Heaven, who has already manifested Himself to us so fully in revelations since the beginning of the world, and above all by the message of His Son. And Jesus our God, Jesus our Savior, Jesus our Model, how can he not know Him?[10]

As for the other truths to be taught to children, Bishop Pasquet lists them as follows:

> If we have no permanent residence here below, do we not need to know where this life is leading us, and if it is to Heaven, to know how to get there, what duties we need to fulfill, what difficulties we need to overcome in order to get there one day? God does indeed grant us His help along the way, but we still need to know about it, in order to ask for it and use it when the time comes.[11]

A child therefore receives from his educator a teaching that will enable him to know his destiny and how to attain it. He will do so through the practice of the virtues. Received as seeds at his Baptism, they are meant to grow, as Bishop André Fauvel, bishop of Quimper, recalls:

> The supernatural virtues, placed in the soul by Baptism, ask only to grow. The child easily acquires a sense of God, of His almighty power and goodness, His providence, His presence in pure hearts. But he needs help.[12]

Hence this exhortation from Bishop Pierre Rouard to his faithful of the diocese of Nantes:

> Since the happiness of your children depends upon their fidelity to the Christian Faith, their initiation in this holy Faith must be the principal object of your affection and devotion, the first goal of all your labor and all your sacrifices. You devote constant, delicate, generous care to their health, their instruction, their honorable establishment in the world; this care is holy, and we bless it, for it is a response to the will of God who associates

---

[10] Bishop Jean-Baptiste Mégnin, bishop of Angoulême, *Lettre pastorale*, 1935.

[11] Bishop Octave Pasquet, bishop of Séez, *Lettre pastorale*, 1927.

[12] Bishop André Fauvel, bishop of Quimper, *Lettre pastorale*, 1949.

you with His Providence. But do not forget, we conjure you, that the true happiness of your children does not depend on the wealth, knowledge or honors they may possess; they will be happy if they are sincerely Christian. You must therefore, if you wish to love them wisely, subordinate everything in their early education to the demands of the Christian life.[13]

This early education is for many the guarantee of their eternal salvation. Bishop Pasquet did not hesitate to proclaim:

> Who does not know that for many, the supreme guarantee of salvation depends on this early initiation? For if there is one conclusion to be drawn from the dangers for youth today, it is first of all the following: that only those whose minds and hearts have been imbued by religion early on have any serious chance of preserving the integrity of their faith and virtue.[14]

Conclusion

The Christian life therefore consists in practicing the virtues proper to one's state. The acquisition of natural virtues and the growth of supernatural virtues are made easier by recourse to prayer and the sacraments, as Bishop Mégnin explains.

> Remaining unfailingly docile [to the practice of virtue] will not be without difficulties and struggles, and that is why help is granted [to the child] if he uses the means to obtain it: the sacraments and prayer; hence the necessity of accustoming him to speak to God, and directing him towards the tribunal of Penance and the Holy Table.[15]

2 – On the Path to Heaven

The main goal of education is to lead children to their final end, as Bishop Marie-Alexis Maisonobe, bishop of Belley, clearly put it:

> Christian parents, do not forget that raising a child means helping him to rise throughout life towards his eternal end, which is the possession of God. When you lean over the crib of a newborn, tell yourselves that God's gaze envelops with infinite love this little being He has given you.

---

[13] Bishop Pierre Rouard, bishop of Nantes, *Lettre pastorale*, 1905.

[14] Bishop Octave Pasquet, bishop of Séez, *Lettre pastorale*, 1935.

[15] Bishop Jean-Baptiste Mégnin, bishop of Angoulême, *Lettre pastorale*, 1935.

> The only thing that truly interests the Creator in His entire work is the lot of the free beings.[16]
>
> Every man, having been redeemed by the blood of Our Lord Jesus Christ, is called, by the effect of the divine good will and on certain conditions, to participate at the end of his earthly life in the very happiness of God. This vocation belongs all the more to children born of Catholic parents.

To obtain the happiness of Heaven, each child is called on earth to accomplish his own mission. God has a plan for each, as Bishop Lecoeur reminded his faithful:

> "We hasten to add," he wrote, "that while eternity is the supreme goal of all human creatures, each of them has a particular end. We all have a task to accomplish, a vocation to follow here below. It is not the educator's job to impose one on the child; he must simply, by studying his tastes and aptitudes, help him to discern the vocation to which God calls him."[17]

---

16 Bishop Marie-Alexis Maisonobe, bishop of Belley, *Lettre pastorale*, 1941.

17 Bishop Paul Lecoeur, bishop of Saint-Flour, *Lettre pastorale*, 1923.

CHAPTER THIRTEEN

Education: A Delicate Art

The role of educators is to collaborate with the action of grace in order to bring children to correspond as perfectly as possible to the divine plan.

In the formation of a child, two elements make his education a particularly delicate art.

First of all, it is important to know that the art of education consists in making the good to be practiced go from without, that is, from the soul of the educator, to within, that is, into the heart and will of the children. "A virtue is solid only insofar as it has penetrated to the roots of the soul and is loved for itself. For this to be the case, it has to be propagated from the soul of the educator to that of the child by means of example."[18] So long as the educator has not succeeded in making the child sincerely say "I want to," he has done practically nothing. The child has to collaborate with his own education, and consequently with the acquisition of virtue.

This is what Bishop Fauvel implied when writing:

> As he grows, you will explain to the child the reasons for the commandments you impose upon him; however, this progressive awakening of reflection must never attenuate the absolute nature of the moral law. You will encourage him to act on his own, but all the while directing him towards the good, never giving free reign to his whims. Until he is an adult and directs himself, he needs to be guided, encouraged or corrected, depending on the case.[19]

This collaboration will have perfectly fulfilled its purpose the day the child, having understood the excellence of the education received and

---

[18] Fr. Jean Viollet, *Le Mariage*, Mariage et Famille, 1936, p. 206-207.

[19] Bishop André Fauvel, bishop of Quimper, *Lettre pastorale*, 1949.

having the Christian virtues well rooted in his soul, will no longer need authority.

Bishop Théophile Louvard, bishop of Coutances, explained this in a pastoral letter:

> Bringing the child to judge his own acts, to become master of himself and his passions in order to conform his will to that of his Heavenly Father, leaves him in a condition in which he can do without exterior and visible authority. Will he not one day have to govern himself, be a man, be a Christian? And there are not two educations, one to make a man and one to make a Christian; there is a single one for both.[20]

Pope Pius XII points out another parameter that must not be neglected in the educator's role. It is that children are never equal, neither in intelligence, nor in character, nor in the other spiritual qualities. This is a law of life. They must therefore be considered distinctly, and their temperament and the conditions of their lives must be taken into account both in rewarding and in correcting them.

Conclusion of the Article

The mission of educators is to help children acquire the natural virtues and develop the infused supernatural virtues, which leads to a progressive perfecting of their faculties and makes them capable of tasting true joy.

In order to fulfill their office perfectly, educators must be balanced, as Bishop Fauvel suggested:

> After the example of Christ when forming His Apostles, parents must know how to ally firmness with gentleness, austerity with goodness, in order to inspire docility, initiative and trust.[21]

The educator's mission is thrilling, but it is also very delicate and complex.

Before considering the persons to whom the honor and charge of educating the child fall, it is important to discern who enjoys this preeminence by natural and divine law. This is the first question we must broach before any other.

---

[20] Bishop Théophile Louvard, bishop of Coutances, *Lettre pastorale*, 1947.

[21] Bishop André Fauvel, bishop of Quimper, *Lettre pastorale*, 1949.

ARTICLE II

To Whom Should the Education of Children Be Entrusted?

CHAPTER FOURTEEN

The Church and the Claims of the Revolution

A stranglehold on the education of children has always been a favorite ambition of the Revolution. Rabaut Saint-Etienne, a famous orator and president of the National Assembly, Danton, Robespierre and so many other revolutionaries proclaimed this loud and clear. They were well aware that in order to change society profoundly, the family had to be transformed, for it is the most powerful instrument for the transmission of values. From this perspective, children needed to be torn from their parents' control. This strategy is indeed the most effective means of successfully fashioning minds according to a single way of thinking.

Authority in general, and paternal authority in particular, were the enemy to strike down. For over two centuries, therefore, the revolutionaries attacked paternal authority, sometimes surreptitiously, sometimes openly. If man, as Jean-Jacques Rousseau proclaimed, "is naturally good,"[22] there is no need for authority, and a child can be withdrawn from the influence of his parents in his earliest years. This also explains the encouragement from the revolutionaries to give free reign to the child's disordered passions.

The popes and the bishops of France lost no time in denouncing the injustice of the State's stranglehold on children. Here, for example, is how Bishop Adolphe Manier, bishop of Belley, rose up in 1927 against the government's unjust involvement in educational matters:

---

[22] Jean-Jacques Rousseau, *A Discourse upon the Origin and Foundation of the Inequality among Mankind*, R. and J. Dodsley, 1761, p. 205.

> Justice must be done to this odious doctrine regenerated with abject paganism, that claims the child belongs to the State and that therefore the State has the right to form as it sees fit the mind and soul of this young slave to a monstrous tyranny.
>
> Nature, blood and love all protest against this absurdity. No, the child does not belong to the State; later on, he will owe it taxes and the tribute of blood, but he belongs first and foremost to his father and his mother, for he is the prolongation of their life, their name, their honor. (...) It is the family that has the right and duty to form the child, to direct him towards the true and the good, in a word, to perfect the life it has given him. It has been said most truly that the birth of a child is the beginning of fatherhood and his education is the continuation of fatherhood. The father and mother are by natural law the educators of their children. Their authority comes from God; it is a sacred thing that commands respect and submission in the home; no public power can confiscate it for its own ends without committing an injustice, and if the public power takes the child to fashion him the way it wants against the parents' will and all too often to entrust him to impious masters, it stoops to a revolting oppression of conscience.[23]

The doctrine of the Church on this matter was reaffirmed the century before by Pope Leo XIII in his encyclical *Rerum Novarum*:

> "The child belongs to the father,"[24] and is, as it were, the continuation of the father's personality. (...) And for the very reason that "the child belongs to the father" he is, as St. Thomas Aquinas says, "before he attains the use of free will, under the power and the charge of his parents."[25] The socialists, therefore, in setting aside the parent and setting up a State supervision, act against natural justice, and destroy the structure of the home.[26]

Pope Pius XI recalled in turn this doctrinal point on the preeminence of the parents over the State in educational matters:

> On this point the common sense of mankind is in such complete accord, that they would be in open contradiction with it who dared maintain that the children belong to the State before they belong to the family, and that the State has an absolute right over their education. Untenable is the reason they adduce, namely that man is born a citizen and hence belongs primar-

---

[23] Bishop Adolphe Manier, bishop of Belley, *Lettre pastorale*, 1927.

[24] *Summa Theologica*, IIa IIae, q. 10, a. 12.

[25] *Ibidem*.

[26] Leo XIII, *Rerum Novarum*, May 15, 1891.

ily to the State, not bearing in mind that before being a citizen man must exist; and existence does not come from the State, but from the parents.[27]

[27] Pius XI, *Divini Illius Magistri*, December 31, 1929.

CHAPTER FIFTEEN

The Irreplaceable Role of Parents

The salutary reminders from the popes and bishops unfortunately went unheeded. The State carried on its work to destroy Catholic civilization with a vengeance.

Society has evolved since, and today, paternal authority has been greatly weakened, when it is not entirely non-existent. What is more, with women often working outside of the home, people who are not part of the family take over the education of the children at a very early age, and this is not without consequences for their future. Indeed, since religion is no longer a priority today for many, children are likely to be educated according to principles that have nothing to do with the Faith.

Thus are parents who take to heart their children's future forced, far more than a hundred years ago, to make the choice Bishop Rouard gave his own faithful:

> In all necessity, either we must resign ourselves to undergoing the degradation of morals, the ruin of the social order, the instability of institutions and a hundred other dire consequences, or we must raise children as Christians.[28]

By watching over the profoundly Christian education of their children, parents are not only working for the family, but also truly participating in the good of society, as Bishop Marie-Etienne Monnier, bishop of Troyes, wrote:

> Is not the Christian education of children the truly patriotic task that should preoccupy the heads of families at present? Children are the France of tomorrow and it needs to be a France profoundly imbued with the sense

[28] Bishop Pierre Rouard, bishop of Nantes, *Lettre pastorale*, 1903.

of duty, a France that is no longer a slave to egoism, passions, disintegrating rivalries, a France imbued with the spirit of Our Lord and the love of His divine heart.[29]

PARENTS' MISSION

The role of parents is not merely to bring children into this world; they are their children's first educators.[30] Pope Pius XII stated this clearly in a speech to newlyweds:

> Christian spouses, your mission in the Church is not simply to engender children for the priests to work on. (...) Along with natural life, you have the duty to preserve and contribute to the development in the children [God] gives you of the spiritual life they receive in Baptism.
>
> (...) In the Christian formation of the little souls God entrusts to you, a share is reserved to you and no one can fully replace you.
>
> (...) According to the ordinary dispositions of Divine Providence, souls cannot obtain a Christian life and salvation outside of the Church and without the ministry of a priest. In the same way, never forget this, ordinarily, children can grow in the Christian life only in a home where the parents, united and blessed by the sacrament of marriage, fulfill their specific ministry.[31]

Pope Leo XIII said in 1880 that the perfection and fullness of Christian marriage is not exclusively contained in the law of the preservation and propagation of the human race:

> There has been vouchsafed to the marriage union a higher and nobler purpose than was ever previously given to it. By the command of Christ, it not only looks to the propagation of the human race, but to the bringing forth of children for the Church, "fellow citizens with the saints, and the domestics of God"(Eph. 2:9) so that "a people might be born and brought up for the worship and religion of the true God and our Savior Jesus Christ" (*Roman Catechism*).[32]

Vatican Council II itself very clearly recalled the constant teaching of the Church on this point:

---

[29] Bishop Marie-Etienne Monnier, bishop of Troyes, *Lettre pastorale*, 1916.

[30] *1917 Code of Canon Law*, Can. 1013, §1. *1983 Code of Canon Law*, Can. 793, §1.

[31] Pius XII, *Speech to newlyweds*, Jan. 15, 1941.

[32] Leo XIII, *Arcanum divinæ sapientiæ*, Feb. 10, 1880.

> Since parents have given children their life, they are bound by the most serious obligation to educate their offspring and therefore must be recognized as the primary and principal educators. This role in education is so important that only with difficulty can it be supplied where it is lacking. Parents are the ones who must create a family atmosphere animated by love and respect for God and man, in which the well-rounded personal and social education of children is fostered. Hence the family is the first school of the social virtues that every society needs.[33]

Pope John Paul II in turn recalled, in his *Letter to Families*, the irreplaceable role of parents in their children's education:

> Parents are the first and most important educators of their own children, and they also possess a fundamental competence in this area: they are educators because they are parents.[34]

And echoing the sovereign pontiffs, the bishops did not hesitate to remind their faithful of this duty, as for example in the following comments from Bishop Cosme Jorcin, bishop of Digne:

> The work of fatherhood is not only an organic transmission of flesh and blood. Man lives above all by the soul, it is by his soul that he is a man; it is therefore above all his soul that he must pass on to his children; it is by the soul that he must live on in them. And what does it mean to transmit one's soul, if not to pass on to others one's thoughts, aspirations, feelings, hopes, faith? Are not the formation and education of the child, according to St. Thomas, as it were a second childbirth, and therefore is it not under the direction of the father and mother that he must grow, develop and receive a decisive orientation for his life? Is it not up to them to mark him with the indelible mark by which they will recognize him?
>
> Yes, the child belongs to the father and mother who brought him into this world, and it is their authority that must preside over his education. (...)
>
> Your children are indeed yours, fathers and mothers; you have received them from God as a sacred deposit for which you will one day have to answer to Him; you possess an absolute and ineluctable right over their education, their intellectual, moral and religious formation.
>
> But these rights that you have over your children create duties for you. God has given you powers over them only so as to impose obligations upon you, and these children are subject to your authority only because it

---

33 Vatican Council II, *Gravissimum Educationis*, Oct. 28, 1965, §3.

34 John Paul II, *Letter to Families*, Feb. 2, 1994, §16.

> is from it that they can expect the protection, vigilance, care and devotion they need.[35]

A child's future truly lies in his parents' hands. God willed it thus and engraved this law in human nature, as Bishop Bernard explains:

> It is you above all, Christian parents, who have a capital role to play in education.
>
> Your voice, perhaps because it is the first to have resounded in the child's ears, is the most heeded; your words are what has the most weight because they come from someone who has the child's complete trust. It is you who have the key to your sons' souls. Evil, alas, will enter in without you, but the good will never penetrate deeply without your action. Even in catechism class, the priest's teachings will be neither heard nor understood nor remembered if they fall as if by surprise upon souls that you have not prepared.
>
> It is so that you may fulfill your role as educators that Providence allows your children to live for such a long time under your care. Baby animals can get by without their parents sometimes a few days or even a few hours after they are born; but the sons of men need the help and devotion of their father and mother for many long years. Do not complain; God has allowed it to be thus so that by the influence you have upon them, by the education you give them, the sons of your flesh may also become the sons of your soul.[36]

---

[35] Bishop Cosme Jorcin, bishop of Digne, *Lettre pastorale*, 1948.

[36] Bishop Henri Bernard, bishop of Perpignan, *Lettre pastorale*, 1942.

CHAPTER SIXTEEN

The Infusion of Grace

As the first educators of their child, parents conscious of their mission are happy to bring him to the church very early for the moving ceremony of Baptism.

Canon law declares that "children will be baptized *quamprimum*," that is to say, as soon as possible, and parish priests and preachers are asked to remind the faithful often of this grave obligation.[37] Raoul Naz, in his treatise on canon law, comments, "It would be normal for a child's Baptism to take place within the eight days following his birth, but for a reasonable motive and if the child is healthy, the baptism can be put off a little longer." He adds, however, "not to do so because the godparents wish to be personally present and can only do so if it is put off a little longer, or for any other profane motive."[38]

It is a question of not depriving children of the beautiful new life that flows from this sacrament.

See what Bishop Julien had to say on the subject:

> The child has only just opened his eyes to the light, when he is taken to the baptismal font and receives, under the infusion of grace that flows with the holy water, a second birth that makes him a child of God and of the Church. A new destiny is added on to the other and constitutes a new right. It is not only the natural food of the body and soul that the child demands, but also the food that will sustain him for eternal life. This is, properly speaking, the right of the Christian child entrusted to his family and to the safekeeping of the Church.
>
> Religion therefore has an important role in the home; the family is the small children's first religion teacher. The crib is their first chapel, their

---

[37] *1917 Code of Canon Law*, Can. 770.

[38] Raoul Naz, *Traité de droit canonique*, Letouzey et Ané, 1955, vol. II, p. 50-51.

mother's knees their first kneeler, whence they raise their eyes to Heaven and speak to the Father of all men. The Church will assist and complete this formation; alone, she would most likely not suffice.[39]

[39] Bishop Eugène Julien, bishop of Arras, *Lettre pastorale*, 1918.

CHAPTER SEVENTEEN

The Parents' Example

As Marie Giral remarks, "a certain number of parents present an image of adults who are not always on top of things. We say they are immature. They do not respect their commitments, do not find solutions, make poor decisions and do not set a good example."[40]

And yet the mission of educator is not limited to giving advice, orders and warnings, or to prescribing prohibitions and interdictions and then distributing rewards and inflicting punishments. It supposes above all the possession of certain natural and supernatural qualities to back the authority of the master over the children. Indeed, the best teacher ever will not be heeded by the children under his care if his life contradicts the principles he wishes to communicate.

Since the parents are the first educators of their children, it is therefore essential that they themselves be virtuous if they wish their children to become virtuous. For their children to become balanced men and women, fervent and holy faithful, they have to strive to be balanced, fervent and holy themselves today. *Nemo dat quod non habet*, "no one gives what he does not have." Pope Pius XII told fathers of families:

> Be models of virtue so that your children have only to resemble you and that one single praise may suffice for them, that of being your portrait. (...) The voice of your example will resound more loudly than the voice of your words: your example will constantly translate in your children's eyes, over many long years, the daily reality of your life. And your children will examine your example, they will judge it with the terrible clear-sightedness and inexorable penetration of their young eyes.[41]

---

40 Marie Giral, *Les Adulescents*, Le Pré aux Clercs, 2002, p. 259.

41 Pius XII, *Speech to newlyweds*, Mar. 19, 1941.

Education can be compared to breathing, the child's soul breathing in that of adults. If the parents have a rich moral and religious life, their children will be nourished daily with their spiritual wealth, explained Alphonse Gaudron, bishop of Evreux, to his faithful:

> Your children listen, watch and imitate. Your judgments are theirs; they will reproduce your acts now and later; your examples will be followed and remembered by them for a long time: Dad, Mom acted like this, let us do what they did.[42]

Fr. François Dantec tells the story[43] of a six-year-old boy who asked, "Is God as good as Dad is to Mom?" This magnificent remark says much for the attitude of this good husband and the influence his behavior had on his children.

But the best education methods will fail if they are not accompanied by examples that form and train wills, declared Bishop Jorcin:

> Realize, fathers and mothers, that your children watch you more than they listen to you; your conduct is a silent but incessant preaching; your works, more than your words, are the expression of your thoughts and your intimate sentiments, and they make a deep impression on the minds and hearts of your sons.[44]

Parents play a capital role in education, first and foremost by the example of their life. As the saying goes, "like father, like son." Bishop Rouard said:

> By striving to sanctify yourselves together in order to sanctify your children, do not forget, fathers and mothers, that to obtain this very desirable result, faith and virtue lessened by the harmful alloy of worldly religious practices and habits are not enough. This alloy weakens the Christian spirit; in the soul in which it is found, instead of the grave thoughts of duty and sacrifice, the dominant preoccupation is interest and pleasure; in daily life, it produces sterile agitation and causes the soul to forget God. In this state, you would no longer be living up to your vocation as Christian educators and you would be exposing the happiness of your children, for, having no vigorous faith in your hearts, you would not be able to transmit it to them.[45]

---

[42] Bishop Alphonse Gaudron, bishop of Evreux, *Lettre pastorale*, 1942.

[43] Fr. François Dantec, *Voyez comme ils s'aiment*, Bk. I, Ch. 2.

[44] Bishop Cosme Jorcin, bishop of Digne, *Lettre pastorale*, 1948.

[45] Bishop Pierre Rouard, bishop of Nantes, *Lettre pastorale*, 1905.

So you see, dear parents, in order to accomplish this part of your task well, you must strive to become worthy to be your children's models. "Be ye imitators of me," St. Paul dared to tell his Christians, "as I also am of Christ" (I Cor. 11:1).

In my own ministry, I once knew a family with eight children who were living peacefully until the day the mother learned she had cancer. She was thirty-nine years old and her youngest was only a few months old. At that moment, as she later wrote, she recalled that "spouses are married for better or for worse." And she and her husband valiantly bore with their children this trial that was as brutal as it was unexpected. She wrote:

> We are living in an atmosphere that is not sad, as some think, but… crucified, in which the cross sometimes crushes us (…). A bit of humor does not hurt, even in adversity, and you have to know how to keep it; it is essential for us!

In the most difficult moments, it was important not to make the cross heavier. She said, "I am constantly careful not to impose my tears on my little ones."

This generous mother understood that the first end of marriage is children. And it was for them that she decided to fight.

"In the darkest hours," she admitted, "I was always afraid of leaving the children the image of a whining, suffering mother… So I asked God (I still ask Him) for the grace to bear the sufferings and sickness with greatness, faith, love, with the will to accomplish His will. Not to be content with the words—so to speak—'do what I say', but to remain an example for them to follow."

But she soon understood that she could not do this alone and needed the help of prayer and the sacraments.

Here is what she wrote a few months later:

> We invariably turn to Heaven… Even the children realize that the solution is out of our hands. We need God's help to carry this cross well. (…) Frequenting the sacraments makes it easier to accept the cross and when the devil, always ready to take advantage of everything, sows doubt and confusion insistently, confession followed by communion restores my hope and my will to fight!

This will to fight enabled her to live ten years longer and to watch the youngest children grow until the day God called her to Him in 2010, on the feast of St. Bernadette.

By bearing this terrible trial with great courage, she and her husband were both a magnificent example for their children. In the end, this mother fulfilled the program she had set for herself at the beginning of her illness, that of remaining an example for children.

"I would like my children," she wrote, "to learn to forge their souls so that one day they, too, can bear the trials that will come unexpectedly."

And she concluded:

> I would like my children no longer to see luck in life. Everything is Providence! I would even go so far as to say that we should no longer speak of good or bad luck like in the lottery… (…) Everything is grace!

This mother had learned to see Providence in all the events of her life, fortunate or unfortunate. That is why she loved to repeat after the example of St. Therese of the Child Jesus: "Everything is grace."[46] May this beautiful example help other families to put the ordinary difficulties of daily life in perspective and lead them to avoid focusing on themselves in the heavy trials of life, an attitude most harmful for the child's true good.

---

[46] St. Therese of the Child Jesus, *J'entre dans la vie*, Cerf, 1983, p. 41.

CHAPTER EIGHTEEN

Parental Authority

I – An Alarming Fact

In the order of nature, the ultimate authority in the family is the father. We shall discuss further the devaluation of the father that has so gravely undermined his authority over the past few decades. It is particularly urgent to restore to him the place he deserves in the family and fully recognize his authority.

However, the mother, too, has an authority over her children. That is why this theme is extremely important for both parents and why we shall discuss it here rather than in the chapter on the father.

In our days, authority is considered an obstacle to freedom, so much so that parents, influenced by the spirit of the times, try to avoid any form of constraint.

Marie Giral describes this increasingly common situation, saying:

> For fear it could be totalitarian, authority has been locked in a closet. No one wants to thwart a child, for fear of traumatizing him, making him neurotic, destroying his creativity. Children are therefore raised by adults who feel vaguely guilty about their authority. The important thing is to be close to their children. Their best friend. The one with whom they will communicate perfectly freely and frankly.
>
> Some parents content themselves with rewarding their children to stimulate them. And these rewards become less and less gratifying with repetition. Not only do they avoid rebuking their children, but they do everything to remove the least obstacle from their path.[47]

Agathe Fourgnaud explains their behavior as follows:

---

[47] Marie Giral, *Les Adulescents*, Le Pré aux Clercs, 2002, p. 260.

> The so-called liberalism of the *soixante-huitards* actually covers up a refusal of their responsibilities towards children left to themselves, disoriented in the face of parents obsessed with the idea of remaining young.[48]

This is not without dramatic consequences for the children. Raised in such a cocoon, they quickly become extremely vulnerable. Soon, they are incapable of bearing the least difficulty or contradiction. Heirs of the May 1968 mentality, they demand an easy life without any effort in return. But one cannot violate nature and get away with it. Raised in a universe free of any constraint, they will have a very hard time as adults facing the trials that are a part of every human life.

There are also children who, to get their parents to give in to their whims, do not hesitate to treat them like equals. The least outing, recreation, or pleasure is negotiated. The child buys it with a promise to make an effort at school or to study hard, and the parents give in out of weakness...

By way of example, Marie Giral says that today people boast of "having a *responsible* six-year-old, capable of staying home alone when Mom and Dad are not there. They are all the prouder of this because they themselves are less and less responsible."[49]

It is surprising, to say the least, to see children deciding how to dress, buying the electronic objects they desire, choosing their summer camp, deciding whether to be an altar boy, or even choosing their school.

Many parents imagine that an explanation will replace an order. They forget that ever since original sin, man is affected in his intelligence by the wound of ignorance, and even more so in his will. Unlike what Plato thought, the sinner is not merely an ignorant man. That is why the light of reason alone is not enough to bring a child to act well.

Today the traditional, realistic, Catholic education that worked well for centuries seems to have been caricatured and even ridiculed. Education has been reduced to simply human, relational elements that did indeed exist before, not as the basis of education, but only to make it smoother. Previously, education was accomplished based on clearly defined principles whose objective was to develop the child's faculties in order to allow him to fulfill his mission here below and earn Heaven. Attention,

---

[48] Agathe Fourgnaud, *La Confusion des rôles*, Lattès, 2001.

[49] Marie Giral, *Les Adulescents*, Le Pré aux Clercs, 2002, p. 257.

friendship, familiar conversations, moments of relaxation with the parents played a key role, but simply to ensure a serene atmosphere in the family and mutual trust between parents and children. Today, reducing education to these relational elements has created the child-king. The result should come as no surprise.

2 – The Origin of the Decadence

This decadence did not appear overnight. For a century now, too many parents have been hesitant to use their authority to form their children in the practice of virtue, which has often led to real disasters, as can be seen from the following warning signs from members of the clergy and Catholic educators during the first half of the 20th century.

The author of an article taken from *L'Ami du clergé paroissial*, dated 1906, began by bewailing the harmfulness of a liberal education in which the child is the idol of the home:

> We are fed on this idea that we have many rights and few duties. It is the opposite that is true. Strictly speaking, God alone has direct rights (...).
>
> Parents love their children more than their children love them in return. The child is naturally ungrateful. You know this, but you are not convinced enough of it. You let your heart go, you make of your children little idols before which you are happy to bow down abjectly. This is one of the falsest ideas of our times and it has been spread by our best writers. Who has not read the beautiful lines by the greatest poet of the 19th century in which he depicts a grandfather in adoration before his little Paul?
>
> "Oh, how that setting sun adored that dawn!"
>
> It may be very beautiful, but it is horribly false, dangerous, anti-family, and antisocial. In the family, the child is the bond, the future, but he remains the inferior. That is the divine order. You have destroyed this order. The child has grown rare in families, and is all the more adored, caressed, spoiled for it. You have forgotten that you are preparing rods for yourselves and that today's idol will be tomorrow's tyrant.
>
> Laws make customs. We know the laws, here are the customs: fathers who no longer have any authority over their sons; children who know nothing and pretend to know everything, despise their parents and their experience and become the ruin, the plague of their house, who, raised in pleasure, seek only pleasure and pursue no other goal in their selfish life than a well-laden table and exhilarating pleasures; mothers who no longer dare to command their daughters, who take no interest in their conduct, who are no longer proud to see them pure, innocent, good, and honored,

> who rather turn them away from their duties and prefer to show them the way to the ball rather than the way to the church. (...)
>
> In truth, God would not be just if He were to put happiness in these homes! (...)
>
> Let the father of a family abstain from ever considering his son as if he were his older brother. And you, mothers of families, never consider your daughter as a little sister. You would be preparing bitter disappointments for yourselves.[50]

Archbishop Chollet, too, observed that many parents abdicate too easily before their children:

> They do not know how, they do not wish to command. They complain they are no longer obeyed. It is true. The cause lies partly in the spirit of autonomy and independence that is so widespread in the modern atmosphere. But the cause also lies in the lack of paternal authority. Very often the source of the crisis of obedience is a crisis of command. Christian parents, do not abdicate, never give in to your children. Let your reprimands be well-founded and measured, let your orders be just. Once given, do not revoke them.
>
> Firmness is one of the best proofs of affection that you can give your sons.[51]

The warnings given in the early 20th century went unheeded, so much so that today, parents bow to their offspring, and their children think they are little rulers, but little rulers who actually feel very alone, for they are left to themselves and have no references.

These remarks are an encouragement for Catholic parents to stay on course in the difficult times our world is going through, not to let themselves be influenced by the prevailing climate, and to return to the natural and supernatural principles that made the Christendom of past generations.

3 – THE EXERCISE OF AUTHORITY

Authority is placed in the hands of parents, who have the duty to exercise it. Pope Pius XI recalled this forcefully in *Divini Illius Magistri:*

> Parents, therefore, and all who take their place in the work of education, should be careful to make right use of the authority given them by God,

---

[50] "Les deux familles," *L'Ami du clergé paroissial,* July 12, 1906.

[51] Archbishop Jean Chollet, Archbishop of Cambrai, *Lettre pastorale,* 1934.

> whose vicars in a true sense they are. This authority is not given for their own advantage, but for the proper upbringing of their children in a holy and filial "fear of God, the beginning of wisdom" (Ps. 110:10), on which foundation alone all respect for authority can rest securely; and without which order, tranquility and prosperity, whether in the family or in society, will be impossible.[52]

Bishop Lecoeur, drawing on St. Thomas Aquinas, explained the nature of authority and strongly urged parents never to abdicate it:

> All legitimate authority is a divine deposit, entrusted not for the good of the one who receives it, but "for the common good,"[53] says St. Thomas Aquinas. It is either a social, or a national, or a family service. Thus do parents, to whom bodies and souls are entrusted, hold from God their power in view of the spiritual and material good of their children. They must never abdicate this sacred royalty, for they will only accomplish their task well if they fulfill the lofty magistrature with which they are honored, with thoughtful, calm, self-mastering and respected authority.[54]

Authority uses commands which, according to St. Thomas Aquinas, are above all "an act of reason"[55] indicating the goal to be obtained and directing wills towards their proper end. Its fruit is peace. It is in this way that parents make sure that each of their children is in his proper place.

In a large family, parents conscious of the extent of their mission are attentive to the needs of each of their children. They moderate the energy of the children with more ardent temperaments who would tend to take up all the room to the detriment of the more reserved. They also need to encourage the more timid by bringing out their qualities. Thus, while remaining firm in their educational principles, they adapt to each personality for the greater good of all.

4 – Necessary Firmness

In order to raise children in the Faith received in Baptism and in the love of God, it is necessary to have clear principles in mind and a firm will to apply them. That is the price to pay if one wishes to preserve joy and peace in families.

---

[52] Pius XI, *Divini Illius Magistri*, Dec. 31, 1929.

[53] *Summa Theologica*, Ia IIae, q. 90, a. 4.

[54] Bishop Paul Lecoeur, bishop of Saint-Flour, *Lettre pastorale*, 1923.

[55] *Summa Theologica*, Ia IIae, q. 17, a. 1.

The child needs to know clearly what is allowed and what is forbidden. He therefore needs to learn the commandments of God and of the Church, as well as the rules set by the parents for the smooth functioning of family life. It is necessary to set limits for him and to be capable of telling him *no* when it is for his good. Doubtless, this is not easy for the educator when he knows that this *no* is likely to cause resentment towards him, but the child will eventually understand that it is for his good. If, however, he is allowed to do everything, he will soon go from being spoiled to being a tyrant. Indeed, as Christian Combaz remarks most accurately in his essay *Enfants sans foi ni loi* (*Children with neither faith nor law*), "youth invents through violence the authority to which it was never subject."[56]

The child also needs to be sustained on this path laid out by the commandments with the practice of virtues and to be subject to a legal authority that punishes infractions and rewards good deeds. It is important, however, to be careful not to act under the immediate effects of annoyance so as not to go beyond good measure.

Steve Biddulph, in his book *Le Secret des enfants heureux (The Secret of happy children)*, recalls certain natural truths in the field of education that are good to consider. He admits that one of his greatest surprises in working with families was to realize that some of the most balanced and happiest children were raised by parents who seemed to him unbelievably severe. The secret was that these parents were severe, yes, but just. They were so coherent that their children knew the rules and the means to avoid being punished. But above all, these children knew that they were loved and felt that they were always supported. For them, rejection was unthinkable. They could sometimes feel fear, but never anguish or a sentiment of solitude or neglect. In short, strict rules and sincere affection; one without the other can have no good results.

In contrast to these severe but just parents, Steve Biddulph met a large number of permissive parents whose children "enjoyed a large amount of freedom, behaved badly without retribution, but felt downright unhappy. Clearly, these children were looking for someone to keep them in line and their parents misunderstood their message. They thought their child

---

[56] Christian Combaz, *Enfants sans foi ni loi*, Rocher, 2002.

wanted more space and more freedom, but the opposite was true. A child needs limits. That is one of the secrets parents need to know."[57]

Claudio Risé, too, recognizes that "the principle of authority builds personality; it is one of the conditions for its development."[58] It is therefore important for parents to know how to be firm with their children.

Firmness is above all the fruit of a disposition of mind and will. Parents who have a hard time getting a particularly difficult child to obey them will do well to recall the following basic rules.

First of all, one must have a clear objective in mind and be determined to apply it no matter what. For example, if your child is in the habit of leaving his toys all over the place and you wish to change this, you must first be fully resolved to obtain the expected result. To this end, you will refuse to enter into sterile discussions with your child; you do not wish to negotiate with him to get him to obey you and you intend not to get annoyed.

The next step is to get down close to your child so that he is looking at you, then tell him clearly what you want of him. You wait until he answers and repeat the demand if needed. If he does not obey, you ask him again to put his toys away, showing him clearly that you will not give in on any pretext. The child will understand that this time, it is useless to try to get out of it and he will do what you ask. By repeating this approach without ever giving in to weariness or to the interior tension you feel, you will soon be relieved.

The first times, it can take a while, and you may be tempted to put the toys away yourself. But if you do not give in and you persevere in this approach for as long as necessary, you will soon recover the time it took and most importantly, your child will succeed in acquiring good habits without which there is no virtue.

Firm parents express clear requests and orders with self-assurance. They are the ones who set the rules and they then shoulder the consequences. They are also capable of patience and perseverance when necessary.

Aggressive parents belittle their child to make him obey. They shout at him, or hit him angrily.

---

[57] Steve Biddulph, *Le Secret des enfants heureux*, Marabout/Hachette-Livre, 2002, p. 80.

[58] Claudio Risé, *Le Père absent*, Rémi Perrin, 2006, p. 20.

Passive parents completely give in. They let their child behave poorly, do whatever he wants, and give in to his every demand.

As for manipulative parents, they use their health, their fatigue or their illness supposedly caused by their child's poor behavior to get him to obey. Remember the story of the mother who told her child, "Leave me alone, you're killing me!" And the next time he went to confession, the child naively told the priest, "Since my last confession, I killed my mother three times…" These parents tend to compare their child to others to make him feel ashamed or to make promises they have no intention of keeping.

5 – Loving Children

While insisting upon the importance of exercising authority, we must not forget that while too weak an authority can lead to a lack of moral principles in the child, too strong an authority can engender a lack of self-confidence. And a permanently negative spirit can make a child lose any sense of initiative.

"A heart is an impregnable fortress," says St. Gregory. "Only affection and gentleness can force entry into it. Firmness in willing good and hindering evil, but gentleness and prudence in order to attain this double end…"[59]

St. John Bosco understood this well, and he used to say:

> If I can become a priest one day, I shall consecrate my life to children. I shall draw them to me. I shall love them and make them love me. I shall give them good advice and spend myself without measure for the salvation of their souls.[60]

Educators will therefore seek to be loved before they seek to be feared if they wish to imitate this saint. "He told himself, 'Make them love you if you want to be obeyed.' He told his sons, 'Do not be superiors, but fathers.'"[61]

If they have to punish, educators should try not to lose the affection of the children entrusted to them. "Put off punishing for as long as possible, and try every other means first; the moment of the punishment

[59] Quoted by St. John Bosco, *Lettre circulaire aux maisons salésiennes*, ch. 1, 1883.

[60] Fr. Augustin Auffray, *Un Grand éducateur, saint Jean Bosco*, Œuvres de Don Bosco, p. 13.

[61] *Ibidem*, p. 261.

will never be that of anger for the master nor that of the fault for the disciple; (…) it will be the fruit above all of reason and the heart and will be administered serenely, calmly and with consternation; and it will be entirely forgotten at the least sign of repentance."[62]

St. John Bosco recommends removing anything that could give the impression one is acting under the influence of passion: no agitation in the heart, no scorn in the eyes, no insults on the lips, but great compassion for the present and hope for the future. By being truly a father in this way, one can obtain a true amendment.

"Lastly," advises this great educator, "always encourage them; (…) congratulate them as much as you can."[63]

As for trust, its role is of the utmost importance in education. It is important to inspire it in the child's heart. "'Without affection, there is no trust, and without trust there is no education,' St. John Bosco used to repeat over and over."[64]

Pope Pius XII declared that "many shipwrecks in life are due to the refusal to trust parents and educators; on the other hand, many bitter experiences would be avoided if we believed trustingly in those who have a greater experience."[65]

Fr. Viollet explains that education is not some complicated system of commandments, permissions and interdictions. While commandments do play an important role, especially during the early years, they will never replace trust. It alone is able to awaken in the child the love for the good that we wish to impart to him, for "education is not accomplished so much through commands and interdictions as through the influence of the educator's soul over that of the educated."[66] And this influence can be neither deep nor lasting if parents do not have the child's trust, a trust that does not imply an abdication of authority. Far from it: a spoiled child is not a trusting child. Severity, as long as it is tempered with tenderness, does not hinder trust, so long as the child has the sentiment that he has never been deceived, that we have sought to help him

---

62 Fr. Augustin Auffray, *La Pédagogie d'un saint*, Librairie Emmanuel Vitte, Parise, 1940, p. 54.

63 *Ibidem*, p. 222.

64 Fr. Augustin Auffray, *Un Grand éducateur, saint Jean Bosco*, Œuvres de Don Bosco, p. 260.

65 Pius XII, *Speech at the National Masculine Institute of Rome*, April 20, 1956.

66 Fr. Jean Viollet, *Le Mariage*, Mariage et Famille, 1936, p. 206-207.

in every circumstance, and that we have given him the encouragements his weakness cannot do without.

6 – CONCLUSION

Bishop Maisonobe gave the following advice to parents to strengthen the will of their children:

> To ensure the moral recovery of our country, young generations need to receive a more virile education. Let us give young people the habit of effort and sacrifice, so that they may be capable of conquering themselves and dominating the material conditions of existence. Let parents never allow them to believe that life is a perpetual party and that the ideal is to live it without any troubles. "Life is not made to be lived, as we commonly say, but to be conquered" (René Bazin). Let us teach the child to use his will, to will![67]

[67] Bishop Marie-Alexis Maisonobe, bishop of Belley, *Lettre pastorale*, 1941.

CHAPTER NINETEEN

The Father, Head of the Home

I – The Devaluation of the Father

The father has a central role in the family. And paternity is not one expression of authority among so many others. It is the prototype, the origin and the root of all authority. Thus, once paternal authority is destroyed, the revolutionaries are sure to be able to undermine all other forms of authority, in particular the political power. That is why this objective was clearly announced as early as the French Revolution.

In the new phase of the Revolution during the 20th century, the attack on the father became particularly apparent in the 50's, according to sociologist Michel Frize. This attack became official twenty years later. Daniel Cohn-Bendit, the principal agitator in May 1968, took the family as his target. "The family," he said, "is a cell in the image and likeness of social injustices." This explains the filthy phrases graffitied on walls at the time, "Rape your *alma pater*!" Or the banners brandished in the streets with "*Papa pue!*" (Papa stinks!) scrawled on them.

Besides the slogans spread by the revolutionaries, other factors contributed to the change in mentality. In order to understand this, we need to remember where the father's prestige used to come from. It was certainly partially due to his physical and moral strength. The father was also considered the one who had knowledge and transmitted it to his children.

But today, machines have replaced man. A father has far fewer opportunities today than before to show his physical strength. As for moral strength, it is so disparaged in our days that to many children it does not mean much.

What about the transmission of knowledge? In the face of the extremely fast development of new technologies, many fathers are baffled at their children's skills. They feel powerless and disqualified. The roles are inverted. The children are now the experts in the technical field and completely ignore their fathers.

Jacques Gautrand makes the following remark:

> There is a sort of infantilizing regression in the face of the new communication machines. The adult, once responsible for guiding the young person in the world, dispensing precepts and advice to help him evolve in his daily environment and become more independent and responsible, today seems to lean on his children's shoulders so they can escort him through the cyber world. Parents learn from their children... in a strange "backwards mimicry."[68]

This inversion of the relation between father and child inevitably leads the child to depreciate his father somewhat.

The revolutionaries' open or covert attacks against the father, the decrease in physical activity for many men, the loss of the idea of moral grandeur among our contemporaries, and the fact that fathers are behind their children in the technical field have all contributed to tarnish their image in the eyes of their progeny.

Consequently, today, "*patriarchal* has become a pejorative adjective, as has *paternalistic*, *patriotic*, and in general all the words that contain the word *father* and its derivatives, that are associated with the notions of backward and unjust."[69]

Paul-François Paoli, aware of the depreciation of the father in post-modern Western society, makes the following remark:

> The Western feminists wanted the Father's head, and in a certain way, they have had it. They reap today the misery of their depressive, lost and neurasthenic sons (suicide statistics show that boys commit suicide in France about three or four times more than girls). They reap the violence that has become a part of everyday life, incivility, lack of respect in the high schools, and schools where women are supposed to exercise their authority but do not succeed in doing so.[70]

Besides juvenile delinquency, the attacks on fatherhood have led to another consequence that it is important to point out: "If so many sons

---

[68] Jacques Gautrand, *L'Empire des écrans*, Le Pré aux Clercs, 2002.

[69] Claudio Risé, *Le Père absent*, Rémi Perrin, 2006, p. 61 and 62.

[70] Paul-François Paoli, *La Tyrannie de la faiblesse*, François Bourin, 2010, p. 86.

balk at the idea of becoming fathers, is it not because they sense that they will be expected to shoulder responsibilities but without the prestige that was once inherent in fatherhood?"[71]

Aldo Naouri speaks of men who "renounce holding their uncomfortable position as father."[72]

Claudio Risé adds that

> the father that is kept from becoming a father (and who is already a mommy's boy) tends to become an eternal adolescent, perpetually seeking narcissistic comfort and lacking in the psychological resources of a man and father.[73]

Every existing authority has suffered from the repercussions of this depreciation of the father and has been affected as much in the educational and professional field as in the political and religious field.

Psychoanalyst Gabrielle Rubin, author of the work *Il faut aider les pères*, declared recently in an interview:

> The surge in what we call incivilities, the fact that justice no longer inspires any respect, that teachers are heckled, and police officers attacked, all reflect a symptomatic rejection of every form of authority. (…) An authority is built based on the father; it is the father who says what is permitted and what is forbidden, who sets the boundaries, who cuts the symbiotic bond between the mother and the child. And he has partially lost his function as representative of the Law.[74]

God Himself is not spared in this war, for He is the perfect and almighty Father. Every attack against fatherhood can therefore only sully His image in the eyes of our contemporaries.

As Claudio Risé points out, "the eclipse of the earthly father, the end of his recognition in society, comes with a correlate weakening of the image of the divine Father in human experience."[75]

It is essential that we be aware of this war against authority in order for the father to recover his true status in the family and in society.

---

71 *Ibidem*, p. 197.

72 Aldo Naouri, *Une Place pour le père*, Seuil, 1985.

73 Claudio Risé, *Le Père absent*, Rémi Perrin, 2006, p. 55.

74 Gabrielle Rubin, "Pas de pères, pas de civilization," *Psychologie*, hors série, mai 2010.

75 Claudio Risé, *Le Père absent*, Rémi Perrin, 2006, p. 27.

2 – The Portrait of a Catholic Father

Families who are aware of the revolutionary process that has led to the devaluation of the father seek to rehabilitate fatherhood. They feel the need to have a better understanding of the Catholic Church's conception of it.

It is difficult to see in one glimpse everything the mission of father entails. We shall therefore define it progressively, by pointing out different complementary aspects of it.

A Leader

Let us first consider how Archbishop André du Bois de la Villerabel, Archbishop of Rouen, summed up the father's mission in the home:

> The father takes on the face of a leader early on, and this first authority imperceptibly leads the child to an understanding of God's. The more serenely and calmly it is exercised, the more prestige it will acquire. Even if this ministry is sometimes misunderstood, it remains nonetheless obligatory.[76]

The first word that comes to the Archbishop of Rouen's mind in defining the father is "leader." It is important to understand its meaning. The father, as the one who holds the authority in the family, is the one who, after prayer, consulting, reflecting, considering, discussing as much as is useful, just and necessary, decides and takes responsibility for his choices. He is also the one who has the final word in cases where there is a lack of agreement, where wills differ, and this is so that the conjugal society will not be broken. In these cases, the other members of the family, and his wife first of all, are to obey him.

In this role of leader, the father must not forget that the caricature of authority is authoritarianism. He is not the one who does everything or meddles in everything, nor the one who decides alone and without consulting. But nor must he fall into the opposite pitfall of non-directive democracy and group dynamics. He must avoid imposing his opinion arbitrarily, but also avoid abdicating in the face of the fickle recriminations of his progeny. He must also know how to take into account his loved ones' limits and not to demand more of them than they can give.

---

[76] Archbishop André du Bois de la Villerabel, Archbishop of Rouen, *Lettre pastorale*, 1926.

Source of Life

Pope Pius XII gave a definition of the father that is more philosophical but no less rich than that of Archbishop du Bois de la Villerabel. He said:

> Being a father, means communicating being; it is even more than that, it is placing in this being the mysterious ray of life. (…) But fatherhood rises higher; along with being, along with vegetable and animal life, it also communicates a superior life, the life of intelligence and love. Man [thus] cooperates with God in the creation and even the infusion of intelligence in his children by the fact that he engenders the body that will receive it.[77]

It is written in the Book of Deuteronomy, "That thou mayst consider in thy heart, that as a man traineth up his son, so the Lord thy God hath trained thee up" (Deut. 8:5). God wishes to have man's collaboration in transmitting, preserving and developing life on every level. That is why a father faithful to his mission actively partakes in the education of his children. He knows that he is the one who is accountable before God, even if concretely he delegates an important part of this education to his wife.

Every means should serve this mission. If he is handy, a father does not simply repair and embellish his house, he includes his sons and develops their talents in this field. He thus educates them to work. He transmits decisive teachings to them by his example: striving for excellence, love of a job well-done, a sense of effort to overcome fatigue. He can also play sports with his boys to get to know them better and also to help them outdo themselves and develop the beautiful virtue of fortitude.

The father has an important role to play not only in his sons' future but also in that of his daughters. Indeed, as Claudio Risé says, the current devaluation of fatherhood,

> this disappearance of fathers, also has negative consequences on the development of young women. They lack the strong, loving and paternal gaze of an adult who, being different, is able to appreciate them and provide an indispensable support for their self-confidence.[78]

In his contact with his children, the father is there to progressively bring them to experience the reality of the world around them with its riches and dangers. They thus learn little by little to evolve while taking

---

[77] Pius XII, *Speech to Newlyweds*, March 19, 1941.

[78] Claudio Risé, *Le Père absent*, Rémi Perrin, 2006, p. 50.

their limits into account. They discover that there is an impassable distance between dream and reality. They understand that if their father cannot get away with breaking the laws of nature and has to respect them, then they, too, have to respect them.

The Catholic father thus seeks to increase the natural life of his children, but his mission must also rise to the supernatural level.

Bishop Théophile Louvard, bishop of Coutances, explained this in the following terms:

> The father is the one who makes this name of Christian a reality. He knows that by the action of God, he is the master, the head, the guardian of the sacred traditions of the home. He knows that paternal love consists in giving of himself, and he gives of himself every day in a labor that wears out his strength and sometimes shortens his life. He knows that he has something more precious to leave his children than the fruit of his work: his examples as a man, a father, an irreproachable Christian.[79]

The father is therefore also the one who transmits more than his name: he provides a patrimony that is not only material but above all intellectual, moral and spiritual.

The ultimate purpose of the family is to populate Heaven with saints. In the exercise of his duty towards the souls entrusted to him, a father conscious of his mission acts under the eyes of God in order to discern his children's true good.

Hear what St. Augustine has to say:

> Let it be for Christ and for eternal life that he corrects them, teaches them, exhorts them, reprimands them, is kind to them, or exercises his authority over them; for in this way he will have in his house the office of priest and even in a certain way of bishop, by being a minister of Christ here below in order to be with Him for eternity.[80]

The father's ambition is to lead all of his children along the narrow path to Heaven, taking up the lead himself. All of his decisions are to be ordained to this end. While watching over the development of their intelligence, their knowledge, and their natural qualities, he also takes

[79] Bishop Théophile Louvard, bishop of Coutances, *Lettre pastorale*, 1947.

[80] St. Augustine, *Sur l'Evangile selon saint Jean*, treatise 51, n. 13.

care of the development of their supernatural life in making sure they have a good instruction in the catechism[81] and a truly Catholic school.

Exemplary and Available

Who can fail to see the need to possess various virtues in order to accomplish such a vast task? Fr. Charmot tells us that

> the father imitates God and Jesus Christ. [He] must first and foremost be and appear to his family as the sacred intermediary between God and the family; he is the depositary of the gifts that are not attached to the supernatural exercise of the sacrament of Holy Orders. [He therefore has to] hold in his hands every possible spiritual wealth: faith, loyalty, honor, work, charity, in order to fill his wife and children with them.[82]

The primary ambition of a father conscious of the nobility and demands of his charge is therefore to develop in himself the natural and supernatural virtues in order to be an example to imitate for his family. When the children see their father rich with such a treasure of virtues, this greatly facilitates the execution of his orders.

Claudio Risé explains that "the father teaches by his example that life is not made up only of satisfaction, comfort and assurance, but also of lack, loss and fatigue."[83]

Relaxing with one's children, playing with them, guiding them in their schoolwork, letting them participate in outdoor work and home repairs, talking to them and listening to them, forming their judgment, giving them a sense of the common good, strengthening their virtues, all of this takes time. A father has to take time for his family, but the hard part is finding it. We often lack availability due to the frantic rhythm of modern life.

That is why Sundays remain an important opportunity to bring the members of the family together. This day that is so conducive to prayer and relaxation allows for a beneficial spiritual and bodily restoration for both parents and children.

Bishop Rouard recalled this in the following remark:

---

[81] "Parents (...) are to ensure the religious instruction of their children" (*1917 Code of Canon Law*, Can. 1335).

[82] Fr. François Charmot, *Esquisse d'une pédagogie familiale*, Clovis, 2006, p. 54 and 55.

[83] Claudio Risé, *Le Père absent*, Rémi Perrin, 2006, p. 9.

> If the necessities of life separate you in spite of yourselves from your children during the week, remember that Sunday is the Lord's day and the day of the family united under His gaze. On this day at least, let your hearts be united for the edification of your children. You will find in this union the sweetest joys in the present and the richest hopes for the future.[84]

A Single Authority in Two Persons

One final point needs to be mentioned to complete this presentation of the father's role. While the father is the principal authority in the home, his wife has a decisive role in the education of their children. In order to inspire their children's trust, it is essential for the parents to speak with one single voice in their presence. They can, of course, discuss things privately and not always automatically see perfectly eye to eye, but they must either come to an agreement before speaking to the child or wait until they have privacy to point out a different view of things to each other. They must not contradict each other before their children, and obviously never fight before them.

As Bishop Louvard said,

> the father has a role by the mother's side in defending the child against his wounded nature. It must always be a single authority in two persons. It would be destroyed if it were divided. It must always appear to the one in whose favor it is exercised as majestic, calm, equitable, and free of any whims.[85]

Conclusion

The attacks against the father have been so strong that today he has lost most of his prestige in his family's eyes and perhaps even his own. It is time to restore his authority to him along with all its duties. This can only be done with a sustained effort on his part and the assiduous and generous collaboration of his wife. Restoring paternal authority is of capital importance in order to recover a sense of authority on every level of society.

---

[84] Bishop Pierre Rouard, bishop of Nantes, *Lettre pastorale*, 1905.

[85] Bishop Théophile Louvard, bishop of Coutances, *Lettre pastorale*, 1947.

CHAPTER TWENTY

The Mother, the Heart of the Home

Ever since most women have entered into the working world, many of them no longer have a clear idea of their role in their home. And yet their mission is both essential and sublime.

The future of humanity depends not so much on rulers as on mothers, for it is they who form men, at least when they have the grace of living in their home with their children and set their heart on conscientiously accomplishing their task.

God gave man freedom not so he could follow all his fancies and whims but so he could act according to what he knows to be true. It is in the family circle, by means of education, that one learns to use one's freedom, and that is what makes a woman's mission so great.

1 – The Catholic Mother

Pope Pius XII told Italian women:

> The woman's function, her way of being, her innate inclination, is motherhood. Every woman is destined to be a mother; mother in the physical sense of the word, or in a more spiritual and elevated, but no less real sense. This is the end to which the Creator has ordained the entire being of woman as such, her organism and even more so her mind and above all her exquisite sensitivity.[86]

The proof that motherhood is indeed woman's principal role is that Eve was punished in this role: "In sorrow shalt thou bring forth children"

---

[86] Pius XII, *Speech to the Leaders of the Female Associations of Catholic Action*, October 21, 1945.

(Gen. 3:16). And we can see clearly that the Blessed Virgin Mary, the new Eve, is essentially a mother, the Mother of Our Lord and our Mother.

It is true that concretely, not all women are necessarily maternal. Some despise motherhood, others fear it. Nonetheless, according to the natural order, in order to fulfill themselves fully as women, all are called to exercise motherhood in one way or another, as Marcel Clément explains in his book *La Femme et sa vocation*:

> Even women who are called to celibacy, whose vocation destines them to professional or political responsibilities, have to fulfill this role of motherhood through the role their particular vocation in the social body offers them on the spiritual level.[87]

Bishop Manier made the following admiring comments on the Catholic mother:

> There is in our midst a creature whose mission it is to preserve the domestic home, to make peace and pure joys reign in it, to maintain respect and dignity in it: this creature is the Christian woman. She is Christianity's most beautiful work.
>
> The Christian religion has made of the fragile creature paganism had debased a being of exquisite moral beauty by fashioning her after the model of the incomparable woman whom we venerate and pray to on both knees, the Blessed Virgin, Mother of God, the sublime model and heavenly ideal of all virtue.
>
> Raising woman up from her ancient degeneration, surrounding her with this respect that is found nowhere else outside of it, Christianity placed her back on a throne of honor in the family of which she is the foundation. It placed in her hands the scepter of an authority, subject, yes, to that of man, but exercised irresistibly through gentleness and tenderness united with courage and dedication.[88]

A generous mother shines in her home by the radiance of her virtues.

> In the family home, a Christian mother is a blessing from God when she bears the crown of virtues that the Church celebrates in her liturgy: the prudent modesty, amiable wisdom, grave beauty, chaste liberty, gentleness, silent patience, fidelity, the long and heroic dedication[89] that are the adornment of a valiant woman and place on her brow a crown of inestimable value.

---

[87] Marcel Clément, *La Femme et sa vocation*, Nouvelles Editions Latines, 1965, p. 29.

[88] Bishop Adolphe Manier, bishop of Belley, *Lettre pastorale*, 1920.

[89] Ritual of the sacrament of marriage.

"Who shall find a valiant woman? far and from the uttermost coasts is the price of her," the sacred author tells us in the Book of Proverbs (31:10).[90]

3 – Educator of the Human Race

Bishop Louvard saw the mother of Moses as the symbol of a Catholic mother:

> Forced by a cruel order to expose her son on the waters of the Nile but clinging in spite of all to the hope of saving him from death, [she] carefully covered with pitch and tar the wicker basket that would serve as his cradle. And when Pharaoh's daughter, filled with pity for the innocent victim, sent for a woman to feed him, it was his mother who presented herself, his mother who was waiting close by, anxiously.
>
> This mother who does not resign herself to let her child travel alone, at the mercy of the current, down the river of life, is the Catholic mother.[91]

It is first and foremost to the Catholic mother that the Church, prefigured by the royal princess, says, "Take this child and nurse him for me; I will give thee thy wages" (Ex. 2:9).

The First Seven Years

Fr. Caillon wrote two pamphlets to help make mothers aware of the importance of the early years for the future of a human being: *Un Enfant de quatre ans est achevé d'imprimer*[92] and *Ce qui compte, ce sont les premiers sept ans.*[93]

Claudio Risé, too, points out the dominant role of the mother during early childhood. He explains that "during the first seven years, what the mother contributes to the child's existence and psychological formation is decisive."

And he adds, "For the same reason, the mother's frequent absence during these decisive years, often imposed by the ways of post-industrial

---

[90] Bishop Adolphe Manier, bishop of Belley, *Lettre pastorale*, 1920.

[91] Bishop Théophile Louvard, bishop of Coutances, *Lettre pastorale*, 1947.

[92] Fr. Pierre Caillon, *Un Enfant de quatre ans est achevé d'imprimer*, Notre-Dame de la Trinité, 1968.

[93] Fr. Pierre Caillon, *Ce qui compte, ce sont les premiers sept ans*, Notre-Dame de la Trinité, 1972.

Western society, produces a series of aftereffects constantly observed in clinical experience."[94]

Cardinal Newman "shrewdly observed that the faults in the early ages have similar consequences to directional errors: a small deviation at the outset can lead to a catastrophe."[95]

St. John Chrysostom, too, remarked on the importance of the early childhood period:

> "From his tenderest youth," God will say to you at the moment of the Last Judgment, "I ordered you to fashion him, to direct him." What will be your excuse if you neglect to do so for fear he will refuse? What will you say? That he is rebellious against constraint and has a difficult character? But you should have thought of this at the beginning, when he was easy to handle, extremely young. You should have imposed constraint upon him, accustomed him to his duty, fashioned him and found a remedy for the infirmities of his soul. It was when this earth was easy to work on that you should have uprooted the thorns, when, because of his extreme youth, they were easy to uproot, when the passions, having not yet grown freely, were not yet too difficult to overcome.[96]

Bishop Louvard drew the following practical consequence that apply to all:

> Leave therefore to no one the complete care of raising your small children; let it be your voice, your gaze, your gestures that imprint the first marks upon them. Or, if you must have help, choose with extreme prudence the persons who will be your helpers.[97]

The mother has a predominant role in the education of her children, especially during the early years. A good influence communicated in early childhood is a foothold that will leave indelible marks.

How to Educate Little Children

It is easy to understand the importance of this period of early childhood in education, but we also need to know how to go about educating our children.

---

[94] Claudio Risé, *Le Père absent,* Rémi Perrin, 2006, p. 13.

[95] Fr. François Charmot, *Esquisse d'une pédagogie familiale*, Clovis, 2006, p. 30.

[96] St. John Chrysostom, *Homily on Widows*, n. 7.

[97] Bishop Théophile Louvard, bishop of Coutances, *Lettre pastorale*, 1947.

The small child is at the mercy of his instincts. He cries or laughs, is afraid or confident, loves or hates, without his will and his intelligence being capable of making the distinctions and analyses required by a moral sense. A child goes straight to what attracts him and instinctively flees whatever repulses him.

On first sight, one might be tempted to believe that one need only give free rein to the child's instincts for him to develop normally. But experience proves otherwise. At first, a child knows only his whims.

Indeed, man is not meant to guide himself by his instincts like the animals, but by his intelligence and free will. And these faculties are not yet developed at birth. What is more, due to the effects of original sin, a child easily follows the inclinations of his selfishness.

That is why all children need to be controlled and assisted by a well-advised authority capable of imposing its will when need be. A mother is thus constantly obliged to intervene, encouraging the manifestations of life when she considers them good and reprimanding them when they seem wrong or dangerous. Unable to speak to the intelligence, she has to act on the child's sensitivity. That is how he learns to recognize what is allowed and what is forbidden. Rewards and punishments are the inevitable means by which a child learns to distinguish good and evil. It is only later on that the child will become his educators' collaborator, capable of loving or hating with a personal sentiment the good they help him to practice and the evil they force him to avoid.

We should add that for his proper balance, a child needs enough sleep and a regular life. Mothers must be careful on this point.

Since the woman is the heart of the home, it is essentially up to her to form the heart of her children and strengthen their will beginning in the early years.

Archbishop du Bois de la Villerabel recalled, "Mothers, full of God and conscious of the grandeur of their task, know how to awaken the heart and fix the will in the good. There are tears she provokes and smiles she deliberately fixes, desires against which she rises up and attractions that she encourages."[98]

Pope Pius XII told mothers, "Educate the heart [of your children]. What destinies, what depravations, what dangers are too often prepared

---

[98] Archbishop André du Bois de la Villerabel, Archbishop of Rouen, *Lettre pastorale*, 1926.

in the hearts of growing children by the foolish admiration and praise, (…) the insipid condescension of parents blinded by a poor understanding of love."[99]

The role of education is to strengthen the will of the child, who is selfish due to his wounded nature. It is by cultivating self-forgetfulness and renunciation that a child becomes able little by little to practice charity. A generous mother strives to help him fight against his selfishness through a spirit of service, to encourage him to help without calculating, and to awaken in him the gift of self.

How to Love Your Child Truly

Through her affection and attention, a woman spreads love and unites hearts. A generous mother gives her child her love so that he may grow healthily, blossom and become a true adult. In order to do so, she has to respect the laws of true love.

Dr. Campbell writes in *How to Really Love Your Child*[100] that a child needs to feel that he is loved in order to be happy.[101] It is not enough to simply impose duties upon him and reproach him when he misbehaves. Parents also need to show him their affection.

For Dr. Campbell, it is first of all the unity between the spouses that allows the child to thrive. He shows that if the child needs to feel loved, parents must not seek themselves in their relations with him, but rather his true good. He makes a clear distinction between appropriate love and inappropriate love.

Appropriate love consists in communicating to the child one's love in order to give him a healthy education and to encourage his emotional growth and self-confidence.

Inappropriate love can manifest itself in possessiveness, seductiveness, vicariousness or role-reversal.

Certain parents tend to consider their child as an object or a piece of acquired property, and not as a person who needs to grow according to his own characteristics and gradually become independent and self-con-

---

99 Pius XII, *Speech to Mothers*, October 26, 1941.

100 Ross Campbell, *How to Really Love Your Child*, Cook Communications, 2004.

101 Dr. Campbell is very lucid on certain defects in today's education. His book nonetheless has serious shortcomings. For example, he fails to consider the influence of original sin in the education of children, the mystery of the cross in Christian life and the role of the sacraments in the interior renewal of the soul.

fident. This is possessiveness. What parents need to do is encourage their child to reflect for himself in order to allow him to forge convictions and understand that he is called to become a person capable of shouldering more and more responsibilities.

"Seductiveness" applies to a search for impure emotions in one's contact with children.

Vicariousness is the desire certain parents have of seeing their children fulfill the dreams of their own youth. If this desire is not satisfied, they are likely to show discontent and fall into the pitfall of conditional love.

Role-reversal is the defect of certain parents who turn to their infants and small children for nurturing and protection. Tired, depressed or ill parents sometimes wish their children to be comforting, reassuring, fully mature and masters of themselves. It is entirely backwards!

To avoid these pitfalls, parents should be careful to have a balanced life on the natural and supernatural levels.

While loving them with an appropriate love, a mother must avoid showing less affection to some of her children than to others, as Pope Pius XII explained:

> There are difficult and rebellious temperaments, but what narrow-minded, stubborn, insensitive child ceases by reason of these defects to be your child? Would you love him less than his brothers if he was infirm or crippled? God has entrusted him, too, to you; be careful not to let him become the reject of the family. No one is so unruly that he cannot be mellowed out with care, patience and affection; there is scarcely a case in which you will not succeed in making some flower of submission or virtue blossom on this rocky and wild terrain, so long as you do not risk discouraging in this proud little soul, through partial and unreasonable severities, the bit of good will hidden in it.
>
> All [of your children] need to feel and see in both your well-weighed severities and your gentle encouragements and caresses an equal love that makes no distinction among them, except to correct evil and encourage good; have you not received them all equally from God?[102]

Forming Children's Souls

The greatest proof of true love a mother can give her child is to help him live the life of God placed in his soul on the day of his Baptism.

---

[102] Pius XII, *Speech to Mothers of the Italian Catholic Action*, Oct. 26, 1941.

Here is how Bishop Louvard expressed this to his faithful:

> Mothers, by the grace of God, you are your little child's first teacher in the Faith; no one knows as well as you how to turn his awakening thoughts towards his Father in heaven, how to teach him to join his hands in prayer, to make the sign of the Cross, to lovingly pronounce the names of Jesus and Mary at the same time as those of his natural father and mother. Thus will you place in his mind and heart the One whose image you place above his crib.
>
> You will constantly show him Jesus, Jesus in the manger, Jesus in Nazareth, Jesus in the Temple, Jesus who sows miracles with the Gospel, Jesus on Calvary and in the Eucharist. Nothing is equal to, nothing is worth as much, they say, as this catechism of the earliest years, however naïve and elementary its form may be. We all owe the best of ourselves to our maternal education.[103]

As mother, a woman is the heart of the home. By her dedication, she is its soul. She can thus have a decisive influence over her child when her heart is penetrated with the love of God.

Bishop Pasquet put it in picturesque terms:

> Remember that a child's first book is, in reality, the heart of his mother, that dictates to her, when she is penetrated with Christian love, the lessons adapted to her pupil's age.[104]

How, then, can she give her children an accurate idea of God?

According to Fr. Emmanuel,[105] one of the first notions that should take possession of a child's soul is that God is the being who is so good that there is no one better than Him. As God is goodness itself, we have to be careful to avoid presenting Him to children as someone who is always ready to punish them. It is preferable to try to give them the gentlest and noblest ideas of God.

When they see something beautiful, it is good to tell children, "God is even more beautiful than this flower, much more beautiful than this diamond, this sight, this view..."

---

[103] Bishop Théophile Louvard, bishop of Coutances, *Lettre pastorale*, 1947.

[104] Bishop Octave Pasquet, bishop of Séez, *Lettre pastorale*, 1927.

[105] Fr. Emmanuel, *Catéchisme des plus petits enfants*, Dominique Martin Morin, 2005, p. 54-55 and 62-64.

When they love someone, we can tell them, "God is far better, far more lovable! So you should love Him even more than your father, your mother..."

By speaking in this way, the educator brings the child to understand that God is all beauty, all goodness, all good, and helps him to have an accurate idea of God.

The idea of God, when placed in the child's soul, brings with it that of the last end and moral responsibility. To help him live in dependency on God, it is important to teach him to please God with his good actions and also to tell him that when he does wrong, he saddens Him.

The child also needs to understand that God is a spiritual being, and therefore a being that cannot be perceived by the senses. To this end, it is important not to identify God with something sensible. We should avoid showing him the crucifix or even the Blessed Sacrament and saying, "See, that's God!" He could take the crucifix or the host for God and imagine that He can be perceived by the eyes of the body.

No, he needs to understand that God cannot be seen, that He is entirely different from the sensitive world. A mother can tell her child, "You have a soul that makes your body live, but you do not see it. It is God who makes your soul live, and through your soul, your body, so you cannot see Him either."

Bishop Freppel wrote the following encouraging words to sustain mothers in their delicate mission as educators:

> If evil has not succeeded in triumphing over us, it is most often because we were fortunate enough to have in our home, in the person of our mother, the first and most competent of schoolteachers.[106]

4 – THE STAY-AT-HOME MOTHER

To fulfill her role as mother perfectly, there is no doubt that the most suitable place for a woman is the home. Pope Pius XII recalled this clearly at a time when women were beginning to desert the home to go work outside of it.

---

[106] Bishop Charles-Emile Freppel, *Œuvres pastorales et oratoires,* A. Roger et F. Chernoviz, 1886, vol. VI, p. 370.

It is a fact beyond all doubt that a woman can contribute more to the happiness of the home than a man. The husband's task is to ensure the subsistence and future of the persons and the home, to make decisions involving the parents and the children; the wife's is the thousand little cares, the thousand little attentions, all the imponderables of daily life that give the family its atmosphere, an atmosphere that, thanks to their presence, becomes healthy, fresh, comforting. (...) In the home, the wife's action should always be that of the valiant woman that Sacred Scripture exalts so highly, of the woman in whom the heart of husband trusts and who renders him good and not evil all the days of his life (Prov. 31:11-12).

Is it not true that it is the woman who makes the home and cares for it, that a man can never replace her in this task? (...) Pull her, draw her out of her family with one of the many baits that strive to win her over and keep her prisoner: you will see her neglect her home. And what happens without this flame? The air of the house grows cold, the home practically ceases to exist and becomes a precarious refuge for a few hours at a time.[107]

To allow women to stay at home, Pope John Paul II stipulated in article 10 of the *Charter of the Rights of the Family*, which discusses work, that "Remuneration for work should be such that mothers will not be obliged to work outside the home to the detriment of family life and especially of the education of the children."[108]

Eleven years later, he addressed the issue again in his *Letter to Families*:

While speaking about employment in reference to the family, it is appropriate to emphasize how important and burdensome is the work women do within the family unit: this work should be acknowledged and deeply appreciated. The "toil" of a woman who, having given birth to a child, nourishes and cares for that child and devotes herself to its upbringing, particularly in the early years, is so great as to be comparable to any professional work. This ought to be clearly stated and upheld. (...) Motherhood, because of all the hard work it entails, should be recognized as giving the right to financial benefits at least equal to those of other kinds of work undertaken in order to support the family during such a delicate phase of its life.[109]

When the father encounters difficult moments in his work, he should not be left alone with his troubles, warned Bishop Bernard.

---

[107] Pius XII, *Speech to newlyweds*, Feb. 25, 1942.

[108] *Charter of the Rights of the Family*, Oct. 22, 1983.

[109] John Paul II, *Letter to Families*, Feb. 2, 1994, §17.

> He needs to feel that he is understood, that his dedication is appreciated, and his worries shared.
>
> The mother is above all the guardian of the house, the sanctuary of the family. Let her devote all her love to making it welcoming; let her create around herself an atmosphere of happiness and peace, but also, in return, may she have the joy of seeing faces turn towards her with a grateful smile.[110]

5 – Conclusion

Society's return to the principles that made France Christian will never be accomplished without Catholic women. While the decadence was principally brought about by the establishment of immoral laws, reforming these laws will not be enough to reestablish order. It will also take the practice of virtue, and on this point, mothers have a key role to play. They are the salt of the earth, the heart of the family, and the family is the fundamental society. In giving birth to their children, they are called to complete the number of the elect. They will do so through the example of their faith and their virtues, after the example of the Blessed Virgin Mary.

Let them meditate upon these words from Bishop Fauvel:

> A mother who does not find in a spirit of prayer and sacrifice the interior peace she needs will never be equal to her task.[111]

Mothers well aware of their mission find their honor and happiness in raising their children in the noblest sense of the word.

Cardinal Pie addressed to them this beautiful exhortation that is also food for thought:

> Sanctification is a personal duty; but if you were to forget it as a personal duty, do not forget it as a maternal duty, as a debt contracted towards your children. God alone knows the influence of a mother's holiness over the soul of her sons. Almost all the great saints had eminently pious mothers. The first grace granted to a man is to have a mother according to the heart of God. The saying goes, "Like father, like son." It would be even better to say, "Like mother, like son."[112]

---

[110] Bishop Henri Bernard, bishop of Perpignan, *Lettre pastorale*, 1944.

[111] Bishop André Fauvel, bishop of Quimper, *Lettre pastorale*, 1949.

[112] Cardinal Pie, *Œuvres complètes,* Oudin, Paris, 1875, Vol. IV, p. 194-195.

CHAPTER TWENTY-ONE

Two Decisive Periods

Among the different steps of a child's growth and his path towards adulthood, two periods deserve particular attention: adolescence and the period after high school. We shall now consider these two important moments in youth. This will not be a comprehensive study on education; we shall simply point out a few fundamental aspects of these particularly delicate periods in life.

I – Adolescence

An adolescent is at an age where the virtue of obedience is more difficult to practice, especially towards his parents. It is sometimes called the awkward age. At this point in life, a young person wishes to prove that he is no longer a small child and desires more freedom. He makes it clear that authority is difficult for him to bear.

Certain parents tend to stiffen in the face of this new behavior from their child and to demand harshly what they expect of him, which only makes the situation worse.

Other parents give in quickly to the unjustified demands of their child or ask his opinion on everything in order to avoid tension.

What is the most appropriate attitude for resolving the specific difficulties of this age?

During this period, parents need to turn a blind eye to secondary issues, but seek to obtain the essential patiently, while using a new tone or even silent obstinacy.

The Struggle of Purity

Catholics know that true freedom consists in freeing oneself from the passions and that happiness is found in accomplishing their duty. But dominating the desires of the flesh is something that cannot be done without a fight due to the disorder produced in man by original sin.

Ever since the sin of our first parents, man has had a disordered attraction for the pleasures of the senses. St. John calls this attraction the "concupiscence of the flesh" (I Jn. 2:16). The concupiscence of the flesh needs to be *chastised*, hence the name of *chastity* given to the virtue by which the soul masters the body and the spiritual the carnal.

It is especially during adolescence that the hardest phase of the fight to preserve the beautiful virtue of chastity begins. Indeed, puberty takes place during these years, bringing with it a certain trouble for both boys and girls due to physiological changes. During this period, young people are all the more disconcerted because they experience new sensations. Their absence of experience increases the danger of falls, and the risk of becoming slaves to this passion if they are not preserved early enough by adequate information.

Chastity consists in avoiding any inordinate use of acts related to the propagation of life and in purity of heart. This virtue thus has a negative aspect, the fight against impure thoughts, impure desires, and lust. However, it does not consist in containing one's senses by reason of an imperative imposed upon us arbitrarily, but in founding this attitude on the offering of one's being to God, and thereby dominating the selfishness of passion in view of a far more thrilling gift. Bodily chastity must therefore have virginity of heart as its source. Chastity is thus ordained first and foremost to a positive aspect, the perfect mastery of the inferior part of our being and the spiritualization of our soul in view of an ideal of generosity. This virtue ensures the unity of man's being and enables him to live a fruitful life.

Teenage boys and girls need to understand that chastity is not a warning against something, but for something. This something is not an artificial oppression of sexuality; it is the primacy of mind over matter, of the gift of self over the selfishness of passion, be it before marriage, in marriage or in virginity.

In order to wage this battle successfully, young people should keep careful watch over their senses and avoid everything that could weaken them in this domain.

"He that loveth danger shall perish in it" (Sir. 3:27). This phrase from Sacred Scripture frequently proves true. St. Francis de Sales, with his habitual common sense, says that the danger of impurity "is always easier to flee than to heal."[113] Experience and all the masters of the spiritual life give the same advice.

The senses are ordinarily the cause of faults against chastity: "Death is come up through our windows" (Jer. 9:21). They are where thoughts, desires and acts against purity come from, hence the need for discernment in the choice of books and shows. Guarding the heart and the senses thus decreases the occasions for the flesh to revolt and purifies the imagination, desires and thoughts. Bishop Maisonobe says:

> Parents are the educators of the child's first purity. It is up to them to remove anything that is a dangerous or unhealthy excitation, to protect his sensitivity and imagination from the dangers in the street, in books, in movies. Not to mention immoral or doubtful movies, the cinema has a dangerous power over the imagination and sensitivity of the child and the adolescent. Through the emotion-filled images it projects, it invades every avenue of the senses, the heart and the intelligence. It overexcites sentimental tendencies, develops a taste for adventure and strong emotions. It perturbs the nervous system and wreaks havoc in the developing organism. How wise parents would be to repress this attraction for the cinema and to turn children and young people towards healthier and more invigorating distractions![114]

Many shows and books also propagate entirely erroneous ideas on the meaning of life and the nature of true love, which lead young people to live in dreams and take away from them the sense of the real difficulties of life, as Bishop Pasquet deplored in 1943:

> At every possible opportunity, theater, cinema, the radio, many newspapers, journals and books, far from praising marriage and the honest family, do not fear to ridicule conjugal fidelity and fertility, while excusing if not trying to justify adultery or free union, unscrupulously promoting the fundamental maxim of Epicurean morality, "follow nature."[115]

All of this is not without consequences, as Pope Pius XII declared in a speech to newlyweds:

---

[113] St. Francis de Sales, *Introduction to the Devout Life*, book 3, ch. 13.

[114] Bishop Marie-Alexis Maisonobe, bishop of Belley, *Lettre pastorale*, 1941.

[115] Bishop Octave Pasquet, bishop of Séez, *Lettre pastorale*, 1943.

> From an excessive freedom in shows and entertainments to a slackening of spirit and conscience in reading, it is only a small step. [Novels] excite the imagination and the senses, and the mind is only weaker and more helpless in the face of the temptations that cannot fail to arise. (…) Christian views and sentiments are distorted and conjugal love is transformed into a purely sensual and profane love forgetful of the lofty end of Christian marriage.
>
> Even when there is nothing immoral or scandalous in them, the fact of habitually nourishing oneself with romantic spectacles establishes the senses, the heart and the imagination in an atmosphere of fancy, in an atmosphere foreign to real life. Romantic episodes, sentimental adventures, a gallant life, an easy, comfortable, capricious, brilliant life, what is all of this if not the fanciful inventions of authors who do not keep watch over their talent and do not have the least care for economic difficulties, and have no problem contradicting practical and concrete reality on countless points in their works? Too much of these writings and shows, even if each taken on its own is not reprehensible, ends up clouding judgment and killing one's taste for real life; it deprives spouses of the wisdom that is developed in them by a deliciously austere life of work, sacrifice and attentive vigilance among the cares of a large and thriving family.
>
> (…) Compared to these romantic fantasies, the monotonous days devoid of any extraordinary events will seem boring to such spouses. For one who lives constantly in a golden dream, waking up is too bitter, and the temptation to prolong this dream and continue it in real life is too strong. How many dramas and infidelities begin there and nowhere else![116]

The choice of one's friends is also decisive in this fight. Pope Pius XII recalled the importance of this to high school students:

> Despite the wisest work of educators, a bad companion can destroy what they build, and in the same way a true friend will strengthen the master's precepts better than he himself can. It is up to each of you to keep yourselves from the unfortunate influence of certain comrades, easily recognized in the opposition you notice between their suggestions and the advice of your educators; but your duty is also to act on others for their benefit. This leads to those healthy and deep friendships between fellow students that grow weaker neither with years nor with distance; they will be the dearest and most precious result of the far-off years of your education.[117]

[116] Pius XII, *Speech to newlyweds*, Nov. 18, 1942.

[117] Pius XII, *Speech to the National Masculine Institute of Rome*, Apr. 20, 1956.

An Atmosphere of Trust with the Parents

An atmosphere of complete trust between parents and children makes it far easier for adolescents to remain open and thus allows parents to maintain a saving influence over them.

To keep this contact with their older children, parents can use activities done together, such as small manual tasks or cooking, to broach certain discussions. They can also cover certain questions during relaxed evenings. This attitude helps keep teenagers from becoming hypocritical. The fact they are sure their parents are ready to listen to them, that they will be there even at difficult times, and that they will be ready to assist them if they fall into certain traps helps them to keep in contact with them or, in the case of a rupture, at least leaves them free to return like the prodigal son. Obviously, this trust does not exclude the parents' exercise of authority or their vigilance and control.

Parents should nevertheless avoid falling into the trap of the modern mentality that consists in asking the child to intervene in his own education as if he were an adult, as if he possessed the necessary perspective to fully judge what is good for him. This is simply utopia. Take, for example, the difficulty of trying to persuade a teenager, and even more so a child, that his work "makes or breaks his future." It is a concept that largely escapes him, for it can only come from experience.

In order to face this delicate period of adolescence, it will be good for educators to remember that while a child spontaneously believes and obeys, an adolescent admires and chooses. A priest once asked a teenage girl who confided to him her attraction for the religious life the reason for this desire. Her spontaneous answer was, "It is the most beautiful thing there is."

A teenager admires and chooses. That is why the motive of obedience has to be replaced little by little by that of admiration. But young people also need to know how to discern the worth of the people whom they trust and admire. When the trust between parents and children diminishes, parents can always have recourse to a third party whom they can trust to take over, be it a priest, a nun or good friends. This is much easier when their children are part of a youth group in which they spend time with admirable leaders and have an easy access to priests, for spiritual direction is particularly useful at this point in life.

Youth groups often have a key role, and even a decisive role during adolescence. In these groups, young people are entrusted with tasks that help them to acquire a sense of responsibility and at the same time understand better the real difficulties of life and of leadership. They learn devotion to the service of others, which is a form of fraternal charity. They also have leaders above them to whom they have to answer, which gives them a different experience of the practice of obedience than that which they have at home. When they are the eldest of a large family, their absence from home during camps also allows their parents to be more available for the younger children. And when the adolescents return home, their relationship with their parents is often better than before they left.

Conclusion

Parents are often a bit disconcerted at the change in some of their children's behavior when they reach adolescence. In facing this delicate period, they should have a comprehensive attitude to try to help their children remain open to them and they should not hesitate to turn to a third party in particularly difficult cases.

When they have received excellent principles during their childhood, teenagers generally get through this grey area in the best condition, as Bishop Jorcin remarked:

> Adolescents, even more than children, need the help of an enlightened religion and habits well-rooted in the Christian life. It is when young men or young women find themselves grappling with error or evil that they more especially need to be strongly armed for the fight and forewarned about the force of their passions. If religious science and practice are not developed in them, their memories from catechism class will soon join their good resolutions and First Communion promises in oblivion.
>
> Here, too, the Church offers effective help to parents conscious of their duty. Perseverance in catechism classes, youth clubs, youth groups, and Catholic action movements strongly contribute to consolidating and perfecting the Christian education of young men and women.
>
> But nothing is worth more than the action of the family; nothing can replace parents' attentive vigilance and the diligent care with which they seek to penetrate the intelligence and heart of their sons with a Christian spirit and form them in the practice of virtue. Above all, and we insist upon this point, it is the example they themselves give of fidelity to prayer, regular attendance at the office of the Church, the observance of God's law, and frequent reception of the sacraments that will be the most active

> means of making their children convinced and fervent Christians and their best safeguard against the attacks of evil.[118]

2 – The Period after High School

Unless they have chosen a different path, young people generally enter college when they have finished high school. A new and important step in their life begins. They no longer have the support of school and their parents do not always continue to have the same influence over them, if only due to the geographical distance between them.

It is time for them to pursue their formation seriously without giving in to the temptation to "live life to the fullest." When they are able, it is time for them to begin transmitting to others what they themselves have received.

For their children to get through this new period in their life successfully, parents should know that spiritual direction and regular attendance of spiritual retreats, as well as participation in a good youth movement and solid friendships are priceless assets that should not be neglected.

Especially at this age, spiritual direction helps in choosing the major direction of one's life prudently and in avoiding certain pitfalls. As St. Bernard says, "he who directs himself is the disciple of an idiot."[119]

And he adds, "I do not know what others think about this. For myself, I speak from experience and I declare that it is easier and safer for me to command many others than to conduct myself."

St. Francis de Sales points out that we are not very clear-sighted about ourselves because of a certain complacency "so secret and imperceptible that we cannot see it without good vision. And even those who are affected by this do not see it unless it is shown to them."[120]

A spiritual retreat at least every two years is indispensable at this age. Indeed, how can one be faithful to grace in the midst of today's world without a profound interior life? And how can one have this interior life without meditation and a regular contemplation of eternal truths?

A good youth group is generally an excellent help for arousing young people's generosity when they join it to give and give of themselves more

---

118 Bishop Cosme Jorcin, bishop of Digne, *Lettre pastorale,* 1948.

119 St. Bernard, *Letter 87*, no. 7.

120 St. Francis de Sales, *Introduction to the Devout Life*, book III, ch. 28.

than to take. Indeed, no matter his vocation, man is made to give of himself. A twenty-two-year-old young man had an opportunity to experience this during a camp that he directed for lack of another director. Upon his return he admitted, "Until now, I had only ever done what I felt like during my vacations. I went to this camp because I could not get out of it, but as the days went by, I realized there is more joy in giving than in receiving." The camp thus enabled this young man to leave behind a certain selfishness and thus discover the goal of life.

During this period in life, the choice of one's friends is essential. True friendship is a friendship that uplifts, not one that drags down. St. Thomas Aquinas, commenting on Aristotle,[121] says that friendship is a love of benevolence and not of concupiscence.

According to the Philosopher, friendship is not just any love, but only a love accompanied by benevolence, when we love someone in such a way that we desire his good. If we do not desire the good of the beings we love, but take for ourselves the good they have, as for example, when we say we love wine, a horse, or other things of the sort, this is no longer a love of friendship, but a love of concupiscence.[122]

It is of capital importance for young people to develop true friendships in the Thomistic sense of the word, both for their own perfection and for their influence on society.

---

[121] Aristotle, *Nichomachean Ethics*, book VIII, ch. 2, n. 3.

[122] *Summa Theologica*, IIa IIae, q. 23, a. 1.

CHAPTER TWENTY-TWO

Parents and Spouses

To conclude these remarks on the role of parents, we would like to add that it should not encroach upon their role as spouses. Indeed, it is important to find a balance between the two missions of wife and mother, husband and father.

At the beginning of their marriage, there is only the first mission, but the second sometimes comes to take up so much room in a woman's heart that it is detrimental to the conjugal harmony. Many wives devote 80% of their attention, so to speak, to their children and forget the attention their husband needs. We are not speaking of a percentage of time here, but rather a mindset.

This pitfall is even more frequent when a man, for his part, is unable to reconcile his professional life with his family life. He has to be careful not to let his professional activity encroach upon his family life. There are husbands who father children but take little interest in their evolution or grow tired of watching them grow up and become teenagers. Is this not a sort of practical neglect of the divine order?

Conclusion of the Article

Christian parents have a sublime mission to fulfill: to turn the little baby, so close to an animal at first, into a being who will one day be worthy to share in God's happiness.

Bishop Lecoeur summed this mission up in the following terms:

> How beautiful is the task of parents who, attentive to the first awakening and first beats of this young heart, educate his sentiments with a

> supernatural and Christian sense, and teach him to love what he should as he should.[123]

Bishop Bernard also waxed lyrical over such a thrilling task:

> How beautiful is this work of education to which you are called! We admire sculptors and painters who transform matter. And yet, their work, bearing as it does the mark of genius, nonetheless remains a work without life; even at Michelangelo's call, his Moses will never speak. Whereas, an educator must fashion and transform souls. Is this not the noblest, most delicate art that surpasses all others, *ars artium*,[124] the magnificent and capital undertaking upon which the temporal and eternal destiny of individuals, the future of families and therefore of the entire country depends?[125]

An artisan is stimulated in his work when he begins to see the result of his efforts. Has God not, in His wisdom, wished to encourage man in the conquest of good with the promise of the reward of Heaven? In exactly the same perspective, Bishop Jorcin invited parents to give the best of themselves in the education of their children, showing them the marvelous effects that will result from it:

> Assuredly, the education of children is a difficult and laborious task. It demands constant self-sacrifice, incessantly renewed efforts, daily dedication undiscouraged by any difficulties or even the inevitable disappointments.
>
> But a great reward, even here below, awaits fathers and mothers who have devoted themselves to this noble task.
>
> The reward of seeing a serious and generous youth grow up at their side, of seeing their sons and daughters formed for a life of work and virtue, prepared to found Christian families in turn or—this would be the most extraordinary grace—to consecrate themselves to the service of God and souls in the priesthood or the religious life.
>
> The reward of feeling that they have carried on to the best of their ability and despite their weakness, the holy tradition of Christians. The light received has been faithfully passed on to those who follow and continues to rise straight and pure towards Heaven.
>
> The reward, when appearing before God, of being able to say humbly, but with joy, that they have courageously accomplished their task as Christian fathers and mothers and to repeat confidently Our Lord's words to His

---

123 Bishop Paul Lecoeur, bishop of Saint-Flour, *Lettre pastorale*, 1923.

124 "Art of arts," expression of St. Gregory the Great, *Pastoral Rule*, ch. 1.

125 Bishop Henri Bernard, bishop of Perpignan, *Lettre pastorale*, 1942.

Father on the eve of His terrible Passion: "Thine they were, and to Me Thou gavest them (...). Those whom Thou gavest Me have I kept; and none of them is lost" (Jn. 17:6, 12).[126]

[126] Bishop Cosme Jorcin, bishop of Digne, *Lettre pastorale*, 1948.

ARTICLE III

Catholic School

Parents do not have full control over their children's future, it is true, for the latter can misuse their free will. But they do have a real impact on their children through their virtues and the type of education they choose.

They have a direct influence over their children when they are in their presence and an indirect power over them when they entrust them to other educators. It is, therefore, most important for them to know to whom they are confiding the care of their children and for them to realize the consequences of their choice of the school in which they will be formed.

We have seen in our first chapter on education that the Revolution sought to compete with parental authority in the field of education, attempting to tear children from their parents' arms in order to form them as it wishes. This project is executed especially through schools.

That is why it is of the utmost importance for parents to know how the State obtained its stranglehold on the education of children and above all, how things stand today.

A child needs unity in his life. His parents and educators need to work together hand in hand. Children should be formed according to the same principles at school and at home, Pope Pius XI tells us:

> The school is by its very nature an institution subsidiary and complementary to the family and to the Church. It follows logically and necessarily that it must not be in opposition to, but in positive accord with those other two elements, and form with them a perfect moral union, constituting one sanctuary of education, as it were, with the family and the Church.[127]

Pope Pius XII developed his predecessor's comments a few years later:

> For children whose minds and hearts are opening to their spiritual need to grow in wisdom and grace while they advance in age, as well as

[127] Pius XI, *Divini Illius Magistri*, Dec. 31, 1929.

> for mothers and fathers who enlist the precious aid of the teacher to help them meet that need, the school must indeed be a holy place for much the same reason that the home is holy.[128]

We have to ask ourselves, "Are secular schools today in harmony with the Catholic family and the Church? And what of the 'official' Catholic schools? Do there exist other schools that offer a formation in keeping with the popes' demands?"

This chapter will discuss these questions, beginning with a presentation of the nature of a Catholic school and describing the Church's judgment on what we call "neutral" schools. It will then go on to analyze today's schools. Next, the choice of a school will be considered, and lastly, a few subsidiary points will be made on the complementary role of families and the State with regard to schools.

---

[128] Pius XII, *Speech to the Overseas School of Rome*, Apr. 10, 1948.

CHAPTER TWENTY-THREE

What Is a Catholic School?

1 – The Church Is Mother and Mistress of the Sciences

By way of a preamble, allow us to recall that the Church is the mother and mistress of the sciences. Bishop Duparc explained this in his speech for the beginning of the 1923 school year at the Catholic University of Angers:

> The Church was born a teacher. She teaches, with infallible authority, the truths of the supernatural order, the inviolable patrimony of which has been placed in her hands by God. It is a mission that she cannot neglect. She teaches, with an authority that has never been surpassed, the truths that reason can know. It is a need, I would even say a necessity for her. She has all the less right to take no interest in questions that are still open for discussion since the profane sciences find in their conformity with the Faith a security that they do not always have in themselves, and since her adversaries, ever on the watch to attack her, never fail to use them against her beliefs. And one of her constant preoccupations is to dispel the misunderstandings, oppositions, and apparent contradictions that a poorly grounded or poorly interpreted science can raise against the Faith.[129]

The Church has a direct, complete, exclusive power over the child's religious formation and an indirect power, because of sin, over the temporal domain. What is more, her mission is also to harmonize the spiritual and temporal orders so that the temporal order may not be an obstacle to attaining the supernatural end.

---

[129] Bishop Adolphe Duparc, bishop of Quimper, *Discours à l'ouverture des cours de l'Université catholique de l'Ouest*, 1923.

In practice, she has the power to see to it that the profane sciences do no harm to the Faith and morals of her children. She can also teach any profane doctrine, literature, arts, or natural sciences that she deems necessary or useful for the more perfect teaching of religion. Indeed, she has the right to use every means useful or necessary to the end she pursues, which is religious education. As such, it is therefore her prerogative to create schools. Canon 1375 explicitly says, "the Church has the right to have schools of every discipline, type and level, elementary schools, high schools, and universities."[130]

2 – Catholic Schools

In order to fully understand the issue of schools today, we first need to know what the Church means by "Catholic schools."

Pope Pius XII defined them based on the end these establishments pursue:

> The efficacy of an educational system depends on its complete fidelity to the purpose it sets for itself. Christian schools fulfill their purpose to the extent that their teachers, both clergy and laymen, religious and secular, succeed in forming solid Christians.[131]

In order to obtain such a beautiful result, several different parameters have to be met, as the bishop of Nantes, Bishop Eugène Le Fer de la Motte, explained:

> For a school to be Christian, it is not enough for it to teach religion at certain hours. Everything about it, its teachers, discipline, program, lessons, explanations, books, and textbooks, has to be regulated by a truly Christian spirit and imbued with Christian piety. This is a truth that many parents have never understood, especially those who did not benefit from a Christian school, but it is a fundamental truth that it is our duty to express, repeat, and preach in season and out of season.[132]

Pope Leo XIII recalled this same principle in his encyclical *Militantis Ecclesiae*:

---

130 *1917 Code of Canon Law*, Can. 1375. See also *1983 Code of Canon Law*, Can. 800, §2.

131 Pius XII, *Speech for the 3rd General Assembly of the International Office of Catholic Teaching*, Sept. 14, 1958.

132 Bishop Eugène Le Fer de la Motte, bishop of Nantes, *Lettre pastorale*, 1930.

> It is necessary to teach religion to children, but not only at specified times. All their teaching should occur in an atmosphere of Christian piety. If it is otherwise, if this sacred inspiration does not penetrate the spirits of the teachers and of the students, the instruction will produce only little fruit and will often even have seriously harmful consequences.[133]

The encyclical *Divini Illius Magistri* would later repeat this:

> It is necessary that all the teaching, the whole organization of the school, its teachers, syllabus, and textbooks in every branch, be regulated by the Christian spirit, under the direction and maternal supervision of the Church, so that Religion may be in very truth the foundation and crown of the youth's entire training, and this in every grade of school.[134]

Fr. Calmel drew the following conclusions:

> Ensuring success on an official secular State exam cannot be the first end of establishments that belong to the Church of Jesus Christ. They have to form Christians. And they can never hope to do so if they do not teach profane subjects in a Christian way.[135]

Why must religion have such an important place in education? Here is how Bishop Le Fer de la Motte explained it:

> A child sees everything, hears everything, observes everything. Everything the child sees, hears, and observes in school needs to direct him in a Christian way toward his supernatural end. How effectively a Christian teacher will draw the child toward the good through his examples as much as through his words!
>
> Education consists in forming habits, good habits. And habits, generally speaking, are only acquired by frequent repetition of the same acts. It is a whole way of living that raises a child.
>
> Water falling drop by drop sculpts a hole in hard granite. A good education penetrates a child's mind and heart little by little. Education is a part of every detail of family and school life.[136]

A child needs to bathe in a truly Catholic atmosphere in order to receive an education worthy of his nature as a child of God. The fol-

---

133 Leo XIII, *Militantis Ecclesiae*, Aug. 1, 1897.

134 Pius XI, *Divini Illius Magistri*, Dec. 31, 1929.

135 Fr. Calmel, *Ecole chrétienne renouvelée*, Téqui, 1990, p. 15.

136 Bishop Eugène Le Fer de la Motte, bishop of Nantes, *Lettre pastorale*, 1930.

lowing exhortation from Archbishop Marmottin highlights this fundamental truth:

> What an admirable conception is that in which the school forms along with the family a single sanctuary to shelter, form, and sanctify the child! Is it even possible, in right reason, to imagine any other? It is certain that in entrusting their children to a master devoted by his state of life to the noble task of education, parents intend to delegate to him the mission that they can no longer fulfill on their own, and that he must fulfill as they would have done. And since the education of Christians can only be Christian, he will raise these children in a Christian way: the teaching, the principles and the atmosphere of the school will be those of the family. (...)
>
> It is by such schools that the children of our country have been raised for centuries under the direction of the Church; it is doubtless mostly to them that France owes her profoundly Catholic soul. Our fathers could not conceive of any other type of school.[137]

For this reason, a school cannot claim to be Catholic if it does not include in its educational principles and its program the elements of Revelation in particular with regards to the consequences of original sin for man and the supernatural organism with which every man living in the state of grace is enriched.

Pope Pius XI denounced this error in his encyclical *Divini Illius Magistri* that we cited above:

> Hence, every form of pedagogic naturalism which in any way excludes or weakens supernatural Christian formation in the teaching of youth, is false. Every method of education founded, wholly or in part, on the denial or forgetfulness of original sin and of grace, and relying on the sole powers of human nature, is unsound.[138]

This conception of education and of the Christian school should influence the life of a Catholic educator. Pope Pius XII described its practical consequences in a profound speech to Italian Catholic teachers:

> Since education cannot be truly healthy and fruitful if content with and limited to the domain of simple natural honesty, your ideal must also be (and is) supernatural. It follows that, just like your private life, your professional activity must be fully supernatural in order to overflow into all the souls entrusted to you. Oh, the exquisite beauty of schoolteachers

---

137 Archbishop Louis Marmottin, Archbishop of Reims, *Lettre pastorale*, 1946.

138 Pius XI, *Divini Illius Magistri*, Dec. 31, 1929.

> who, first thing in the morning, spent time with God in prayer and the meditation of divine things, fed on the flesh of the Immaculate Lamb, and who, ardent and radiant, take in hand these intelligences and hearts of little baptized souls to whom they communicate paternally and maternally their spiritual wealth![139]

---

[139] Pius XII, *Speech at the Frances Xavier Cabrini Institute*, Apr. 29, 1945.

CHAPTER TWENTY-FOUR

The Attacks on the Catholic School

Given the influence of Catholic schools on children, the enemies of the Church have done everything to fight against them methodically.

I – "Neutral Schools"

We saw in the chapter entitled "To Whom Should the Education of Children Be Entrusted?" that the State's stranglehold on childhood is a plan that dates back to the Revolution. Bishop Pasquet explained this to his faithful, describing the different steps that led to the creation of "neutral schools":

> Ever since the Revolution, we can say, the school system in France has step by step developed as the consequence of this principle, asserted more clearly day by day: take the child, who will be a gear in tomorrow's national organism; take him at the age where he is particularly susceptible to be influenced so as to raise him away from any religious life that the State claims to be incompetent to give him. And in this way, they now hope to organize humanity without God, just as the Church once formed Christendom by means of religion.
>
> The pursuit of this program was obviously adapted to the circumstances, accelerated or slowed down depending on whether the public conscience approved or opposed it. But throughout the entire century, the goal remained the same.[140]

The bishop of Séez offered a few examples to support these remarks:

---

[140] Bishop Octave Pasquet, bishop of Séez, *Lettre pastorale*, 1928.

> When the Convention decided[141] that the nation, "the common mother of all citizens," should "take man from his crib" to raise him "in national houses"; when Monsieur Cousin, opposed to the freedom to teach, called this right a "public power that the law alone can confer,"[142] both cases were already an affirmation of the same purpose that later brought Waldeck-Rousseau to wish to allow in France "only a single type of youth,"[143] withdrawn, of course, from the action of the Church that was to be handed over irrevocably to the dictatorship of official instruction.

Every Catholic conscious of his duties spontaneously rejects evil. He cannot bear to see his children receive an instruction that openly attacks Faith or morals. Therefore, the secularists played the card of neutrality to reassure Catholics and thus lay hands on the youth.

In his 1936 pastoral letter, Bishop Mégnin enlightened the faithful of his diocese as to the nature of these so-called neutral schools:

> The neutral school is, by definition, a school that does not take sides, that eliminates from its programs any religious teaching and forbids its teachers, on principle, any words or acts that could offend or attack the beliefs of its students and their families.
>
> For over fifty years now, in France, it has been the only school of the State. At first it preserved, at least in practice, the fundamental notions on God and the soul. It had ceased to be Christian but was not yet entirely a-religious. We still remember a little textbook on morality that the teacher placed in our hands around the year 1890; there was still a chapter (the last) dedicated to God and man's duties towards Him. Up until 1889, our classes began with the recitation of a prayer, and we can still hear the teacher's grave words announcing to us that this exercise would no longer take place. But little by little, every last trace of religious formation disappeared, and for a long time now, the name of God has ceased to be pronounced in lessons. He has been erased from school textbooks. Religion has been entirely excluded.[144]

2 – The Utopia of Neutrality in Schools

Neutrality is a sophism that needs to be unmasked, as Bishop Nègre, Bishop Mégnin, and Bishop Le Fer de la Motte did not hesitate to do.

---

141 Rabaut Saint-Etienne, Dec. 21, 1792.

142 Debates from April 22 to May 24, 1844.

143 October 20, 1900.

144 Bishop Jean-Baptiste Mégnin, bishop of Angoulême, *Lettre pastorale*, 1936.

Promoters of "neutral schools" insist upon the good in them, but carefully avoid mentioning their deficiencies, the bishop of Tours, Bishop Albert Nègre, reminded his faithful:

> We must not fail to point out that these schools present themselves under appearances of honesty, and that too many Catholics let themselves be deceived by these false appearances. "Why such a harsh judgment on neutral schools?" say those who defend them. "See what they teach: reading, writing, history, geography, spelling, math, *etc.* Is there anything wrong with these things? No. So why do you call these schools bad, since what they teach is good? And everything bad is excluded. It is forbidden to pronounce a single word against religion or say a single word that could offend morality. These schools are irreproachable."
>
> We have here a beautiful argument in favor of neutral schools, and yet it is false and fallacious.
>
> Why? Because this argument shows what is good in these schools and hides what is bad. The outer clothing covers the cancer. Neutral schools sin by omission.[145]

Indeed, in "neutral schools," educators disregard the disorder in human nature due to original sin, which leads to grave deficiencies in the education of children, as Bishop Mégnin explained:

> [Education] includes a moral formation. Our Faith teaches us that while Baptism erases original sin, it leaves tendencies to evil in Christians. And does not simple experience show that with the first use of reason grave defects in every domain are already revealed in human nature? "Disorderly inclinations then," says Pius XI, "must be corrected, good tendencies encouraged and regulated from tender childhood."[146]

Hence the necessity of imparting the notion of duty both towards oneself and towards others, beginning with parents and one's neighbor. But duty implies obligation, and obligation implies constraint, renunciation, sacrifices that have to be repeated all throughout one's existence.

Once religion is abandoned, the teacher no longer has any untouchable principles in whose name to demand of the child the necessary efforts for his formation, added the bishop of Angoulême:

> In the name of what principles can an educator impose a moral law that represses the passions and demands constant efforts?

---

145 Bishop Albert Nègre, bishop of Tours, *Lettre pastorale*, 1928.

146 Pius XI, *Divini Illius Magistri*, Dec. 31, 1929.

> In the name of the conscience? The conscience is soon stifled if it is not presented as the imperative voice of God, witness today and judge tomorrow.
>
> In the name of interest? Interest varies with each individual's conception of it.
>
> In the name of solidarity? It is a feeble rampart when it is not based on charity that unites the children of the same Father in Heaven.
>
> In the name of society? But what gives one man a right to command another, if he does not hold his authority from a superior authority, that of God?
>
> There remain exterior punishments. Purely servile fear does not educate. The duty towards God is the foundation of all other duties. No moral formation worthy of the name can be accomplished if it is not based on the knowledge of God, of the spiritual and immortal soul, and of the afterlife in which all justice will be fulfilled in the reward or chastisement distributed by the Sovereign Judge.[147]

"Neutral schools" also neglect to raise man to the supernatural order through sanctifying grace. They have a rationalistic approach to teaching. But the history of France, for example, is so closely connected with the history of the Church that it is impossible to teach it without taking a stance on religious events.

We can meditate upon these beautiful remarks from Bishop Le Fer de la Motte:

> How can a neutral schoolteacher teach history, the history of France, which is none other than the story of God's actions in our country—*gesta Dei per Francos*? How can he speak of Clovis and the Christian vocation of our country, the Crusades, St. Louis and the "very Christian kings," Joan of Arc and her divine mission, the flowers of sanctity that made France? He will have to erase the name of God, that name that shines on every page of our history, and present as vain and imaginary the cry of our fathers, "Long live Christ who loves the Franks!"[148]

The study of literature and philosophy cannot exclude the spiritual and even Christian aspect either, for it is necessarily included.

Bishop Mégnin concluded with this crucial question:

> Will a child who has sensed in his teacher ideas contrary to the teachings of the Catholic religion, who has heard him make declarations and

[147] Bishop Jean-Baptiste Mégnin, bishop of Angoulême, *Lettre pastorale*, 1936.

[148] Bishop Eugène Le Fer de la Motte, bishop of Nantes, *Lettre pastorale*, 1927.

judgments that trouble his faith, go joyfully and with all his heart from school to catechism class?[149]

3 – THE EXTENT OF THE HARM DONE BY "NEUTRAL SCHOOLS"

Pope Pius XII says that "officially neutral instruction does not form and often deforms minds."[150]

Bishop Mégnin explained why:

> For several hours a day, a student absorbs a teaching that totally and systematically excludes any religious notion. In the formation he receives at school, not one of these strengths, these spiritual values that we have concretely defined are mentioned. We should add that the teacher has great prestige in the child's eyes, the prestige that comes with knowledge and authority. And for two or three hours a week, the same child hears lessons from a priest who imparts to him the great Christian doctrine that should inspire and fill his entire life. In sum, two different conceptions of his existence are offered to him: one is naturalistic, the other steeped in the supernatural.
>
> Does the former prepare the latter? If religion is of capital importance, the child will tell himself, if it corresponds to a reality, why does my teacher exclude it from his teaching and advice? And doubt grazes his mind, a beginning of skepticism is likely to take hold of him; he will not go to the priest's lessons with an open and receptive heart and mind. (...)
>
> This apprehension is even more distressing in the face of another possibility, that of the violation of neutrality.[151]

And this principle is very frequently violated, for, as Pope Pius XI said, "a 'neutral' or 'lay' school, from which religion is excluded… cannot exist in practice; it is bound to become irreligious."[152]

A teaching that excludes God as a matter of principle cannot but deform children's judgment and lead them to materialism and atheism, against which Bishop Le Fer de la Motte warned:

---

149 Bishop Jean-Baptiste Mégnin, bishop of Angoulême, *Lettre pastorale*, 1936.

150 Pius XII, *Radio Message for the 4th Inter-American Congress of Catholic Education*, Aug. 5, 1951.

151 Bishop Jean-Baptiste Mégnin, bishop of Angoulême, *Lettre pastorale*, 1936.

152 Pius XI, *Divini Illius Magistri*, Dec. 31, 1929.

> School neutrality presents an unacceptable vice that we must have the courage to point out and recognize. It is a tall order to try to teach natural science and speak of heaven and earth without encountering and adoring their Author! How poor it is to speak of duty and morality without seeking and teaching their true foundation, their Judge, their sanction and obligatory principle! In speaking of the human body without mentioning its immortal soul, of life without blessing the first source of all living beings, of death without answering or even asking the question of the afterlife, one proves incapable of satisfying the legitimate and touching curiosity of the child who badgers us with his questions: "And then what? And why?" One locks him up within the limited circle of that which can be seen, felt or heard; in other words, one accustoms him to live in a practical materialism bereft of any ideal or eternal hope.[153]

One of the promoters of this type of school wrote, "A school without God is a school against God. We cannot do anything about it; that's the way it is."[154]

As Bishop Freppel pointed out, "a child who for six years spends five hours a day at school without ever hearing God mentioned will have no difficulty believing that God does not exist, or that He can be disregarded."[155]

During the same years, the bishops also condemned mixed-sex education in schools that was imposed by Freemasonry, as Bishop Manier explained:

> As early as 1905, the lodges voiced this wish: "That mixed-sex education may be applied to all primary schools, even normal schools, and that at the head of each co-ed school may be placed a married or unmarried couple."
>
> More recently, the 1923 Convention asked for "a single primary school system to be created and made obligatory for all children without any distinction between the sexes." And the requests of Freemasonry are always accepted and accomplished. (…) In a certain number of schools, there is no longer any distinction between the classes of boys and the classes of girls. This immoral promiscuity is unacceptable. (…)
>
> We shall [consequently] fight with enduring energy against immoral coeducation.[156]

---

153 Bishop Eugène Le Fer de la Motte, bishop of Nantes, *Lettre pastorale*, 1930.

154 *Revue de l'Enseignement primaire*, 1909.

155 Bishop Charles-Emile Freppel, *Œuvres pastorales et oratoires*, A. Roger et F. Chernoviz, 1902, vol. V, p. 237-238.

156 Bishop Adolphe Manier, bishop of Belley, *Lettre pastorale*, 1927.

Pope Pius XI wrote two years later that coeducation is founded on naturalism, which denies original sin:

> [Coeducation], too, is founded upon a deplorable confusion of ideas that mistakes a leveling promiscuity and equality, for the legitimate association of the sexes. The Creator has ordained and disposed perfect union of the sexes only in matrimony, and, with varying degrees of contact, in the family and in society. Besides there is not in nature itself, which fashions the two quite different in organism, in temperament, in abilities, anything to suggest that there can be or ought to be promiscuity, and much less equality, in the training of the two sexes. These, in keeping with the wonderful designs of the Creator, are destined to complement each other in the family and in society, precisely because of their differences, which therefore ought to be maintained and encouraged during their years of formation, with the necessary distinction and corresponding separation, according to age and circumstances. These principles, with due regard to time and place, must, in accordance with Christian prudence, be applied to all schools, particularly in the most delicate and decisive period of formation.[157]

"Neutral schools" are largely responsible for the lack of vocations, observed Archbishop Marmottin:

> How could the child who, we suppose, has a priestly vocation, not lose, over the course of his years in school, and sense and love of the supernatural? How could the small flame, the divine ideal once lit in his soul, not flicker and die out? The rare catechism lessons he receives elsewhere, and the influence of an insufficiently Christian family will not be enough to keep it alive. We should not be surprised at the increasing drop in vocations in our rural areas. And notice that the dioceses that are still rich in priests are those where there is a large number of free schools.[158]

"Neutral schools" do not wreak havoc only among children; their repercussions affect even families and civil society.

Bishop Nègre decried these disorders:

> Doubtless when the Roman Congregations and the popes unmask for us the evil of these condemned schools, they target above all the danger of perversion they necessarily present for the faith and morals of children. The Church seeks above all to preserve the innocent souls of her dear baptized children, innocent, trusting, and defenseless lambs. But she does not remain altogether silent as to the profound disorders that flow from these schools

---

157 Pius XI, *Divini Illius Magistri*, Dec. 31, 1929.

158 Archbishop Louis Marmottin, archbishop of Reims, *Lettre pastorale*, 1954.

> onto families and into society. It would be an incomplete conception of the evils of "neutral schools" to consider only their effects on children, even though they are their first victims. Indeed, public schools from which all religion and any true rule of honesty are banished by an essentially impious and immoral law, tend to overthrow the social order. They are essentially opposed to justice and violate every right.[159]

4 – The Role Played by Freemasonry

After so many testimonies to the harmful nature of "neutral schools" from the highest authorities in the Church of France, it is time to take a look at the avowals of the very men who promoted these schools, as revealed here and there by the bishops of the last century:

> In reality, the declarations made by those who propagate neutrality are abominably false. We do not even need to say it. The most official leaders of free thought have coldly admitted it. Hear what they have to say.
>
> "No ambiguity. Let us no longer say we do not wish to destroy religion; let us rather say we wish to destroy religion."[160]

"'School without God; they throw this label in our faces to accuse us. We assert it as an honorary title. It expresses our very purpose...'[161] Thus spoke Monsieur Guery, Academy Inspector."[162]

Monsieur Viviani's avowal to the French tribune is worth remembering: "They talk of school neutrality. But it is time to say that school neutrality has never been anything more than a diplomatic lie to suit the circumstances."[163]

Brother Dequaire-Grobel, Academy Inspector, said at a Convention of the Grand Orient in 1896:

> The goal of lay schools is not to teach students to read, write, and count, but to form free thinkers.
>
> When he leaves the school benches at the age of thirteen, a student who still believes has not benefited from the teaching he has received.
>
> Lay schools only bear fruit if the child is rid of dogma, if he has denied the Faith of his fathers, if he has renounced the Catholic Faith.

---

159 Bishop Albert Nègre, bishop of Tours, *Lettre pastorale*, 1928.

160 Aulard, *Jeunesse laïque*, Aug. 10, 1924, p. 36.

161 Guery, *Revue de l'Enseignement primaire*, Jan. 27, 1907.

162 Bishop Eugène Le Fer de la Motte, bishop of Nantes, *Lettre pastorale*, 1927.

163 *Journal Officiel*, Jan. 18, 1890.

> Lay schools are a mold into which you put the son of a Christian and from which comes a renegade.
>
> Since things are not going quickly enough for our taste to make the apostasy more general, we shall take over the monopoly of education and families will be forced to hand their children over to us.[164]

In the face of the determination with which Christian schools were attacked at the end of the 19th century, the bishops of France did not hesitate to denounce the Freemasonic conspiracy.

Thus did Bishop Le Fer de la Motte declare in 1927 that lay schools were of Masonic origin.

> In the present struggle against the Christianization of children," he declared, "it is impossible not to see a Masonic origin. A synoptic table of Masonic decisions and legal acts against Christian schools has been drawn up. It is suggestive and entirely convincing.[165]

After denouncing Freemasonry's rule in the establishment of lay schools, the bishop of Nantes quoted the declarations of the members themselves:

> The avowal of the Freemasons is a known fact. One has only to listen to what they have to say.
>
> "We are the front lines of lay and Republican education. Wherever there is a child, wherever there is a school, you will find the hand of a Freemason, so that the famous saying—Masonry and education are one and the same thing—may become a reality."[166]

> Lay and obligatory instruction was studied, prepared and, so to speak, decreed in the Lodges many years ago; that is what made it possible for it to be voted in by the Chamber.[167]

There you have the war plan against Christian schools, a plan that seeks to attack God Himself:

---

164 Archbishop André du Bois de la Villerabel, archbishop of Rouen, *Lettre pastorale*, 1926.

165 Bishop Eugène Le Fer de la Motte, bishop of Nantes, *Lettre pastorale*, 1927.

166 1879 Convention, quoted in *La Chaîne de l'union.*

167 *Le Mot d'ordre,* May 1885.

> At the solstice celebration of the *Clémente amitié*, Monsieur de Lanessan, a former minister, declared unequivocally: "We wish to crush in the infamous thing, and the infamous thing is God."[168] [169]

Bishop Le Fer de la Motte went on to list and describe the laws that were voted in to execute the Masonic plan:

> – Article 7 of the law of 1879 forbade unauthorized congregations to teach.
> – The law of 1882 expelled religion from the official school programs.
> – The law of 1886 secularized the teaching staff of public schools.
> – The law of 1904 declared any member of a religious congregation unfit to teach.
>
> And so on. And we should not fail to add that even after the Great War, the *Official Journal* announced on February 25, 1923 that "the duties towards God as conscience and reason can reveal them" had been removed from school programs.[170]

5 – Practical Consequences

This lengthy development on the true nature of "neutral schools" leads us to the conclusion Bishop Nègre gave his faithful of the diocese of Tours:

> Neutral schools are therefore evil, very evil, they are to be condemned and avoided. This has been proven. Common sense, reason, and the authority of the Church leave no doubt on the question. On such a grave issue, it was important neither to exaggerate the evil, nor to cover up any of its aspects.[171]

Twenty years earlier, the same bishop, then at the head of the see of Tulle, had prescribed an extremely radical remedy for these schools at the beginning of one of his pastoral letters:

> What a deadly illusion to hope that neutral schools will do little or no evil! A bad tree always gives bad fruit; it cannot be healed, and the only way to be rid of the poisonous fruit is to strike it down at the root. Our Lord gave this remedy along with the condemnation: the evil tree will be

---

168 *Le Monde Maçonnique*, Apr. 1880, p. 502.

169 Bishop Eugène Le Fer de la Motte, bishop of Nantes, *Lettre pastorale*, 1927.

170 *Ibidem.*

171 Bishop Albert Nègre, bishop of Tours, *Lettre pastorale*, 1928.

> cut down and cast into the fire (Mt. 7:17-19). It is no reckless audacity to tell you these things, but a simple duty of our pastoral charge.[172]

In this judgment that may appear severe, the prelate was really only drawing the practical conclusions of the teaching of Popes Pius IX and Leo XIII.

In his encyclical *Nobilissima Gallorum Gens*,[173] addressed to the French nation, Leo XIII wrote:

> The Church, guardian of the integrity of the Faith, who, by virtue of her authority, deputed from God her Founder, has to call all nations to the knowledge of Christian lore, and who is consequently bound to watch keenly over the teaching and upbringing of the children placed under her authority by Baptism, has always expressly condemned mixed or neutral schools; over and over again she has warned parents to be ever on their guard on this most essential point.[174]

As early as 1866, after a law on education was passed, the bishops of Switzerland had asked the pope, through the intermediary of the Congregation of the Holy Office, if parents were allowed to send their children to "neutral schools." The Holy Office answered that this solution was out of the question:

> In examining this question, the Most Eminent Fathers have been struck by the intrinsic danger attached to these schools (...). They have judged that everything must be done to convince fathers of families that there is nothing worse they can do against their children, their country and Catholic interests than to throw their sons into this extreme danger.[175]

The *1917 Code of Canon Law* stipulates the following measures to protect children and avoid any danger of corrupting them:

> Catholic children shall not frequent non-Catholic, neutral, or mixed schools that are also open to non-Catholics. Only the local Ordinary can tolerate frequenting such schools, according to the guidelines in the instruc-

---

172 Bishop Albert Nègre, bishop of Tulle, *Lettre pastorale*, 1909.

173 Translation: the most noble French nation.

174 Leo XIII, *Nobilissima Gallorum Gens*, Feb. 8, 1884.

175 Instruction of the Holy Office to the bishops of Switzerland on neutral schools, March 6, 1866, "Congrégations Romaines," *L'Ami du clergé*, Oct. 3, 1901.

> tions from the Holy See, after taking the necessary measures to compensate and the necessary precautions to avoid any danger of perversion.[176]

The bishops did indeed tolerate exceptions to the rule we have just presented and laid out certain conditions to be respected. There has to be a grave motive and the parents have to take every precaution capable of diminishing the danger. One of these two conditions is not enough; both must necessarily be respected simultaneously.

Here is what Bishop Mégnin had to say on the question:

> Parents who, for various reasons, cannot send their children to boarding school, (...) have no other resource but the official—that is to say, neutral or secular—schools. (...) The bishops of France have therefore defined the guarantees [required in this case]: "Nothing in these schools must present an attack on the child's conscience; the parents must also supply outside of class the religious instruction and formation that students cannot receive in class."(...)
>
> [As far as] the dangers for the students' consciences go, (...) there can be danger for the Faith and danger for morals, that can come either from the moral teachings or from the books or from the methods.
>
> (...) If your vigilance reveals to you that the school in which you have been obliged to place your child is not neutral, you will first address the matter with the teacher, without bitterness, but firmly. If your remarks are not taken into consideration, if the faith of your children truly is in real danger, no consideration can dispense you from the duty to tear your son or your daughter away from such a place.
>
> "First and foremost, his soul must be saved." These are the final words of the warning given to Christian parents by the French episcopate in 1934.[177]

We shall now consider the formation received in the different types of schools today, in order to enlighten parents on this question that is so essential for their children's future.

---

[176] *1917 Code of Canon Law,* Can. 1374.

[177] Bishop Jean-Baptiste Mégnin, bishop of Angoulême, *Lettre pastorale,* 1936.

CHAPTER TWENTY-FIVE

Schools Today

After defining the nature of Catholic schools and considering the warnings from the hierarchy of the Church against so-called neutral schools, here is a small presentation of the different forms of schools in which parents can enroll their children today.

Parents have the choice today between public schools, official Catholic schools, and free Catholic schools. They can also homeschool, with the help of homeschool programs, for example.

Both types of Catholic schools were born in France of the Debré Law in 1959. For the moment, let us take a look at subsidized private schools. Fully Catholic schools will be discussed further on in the chapter entitled "What School for Our Children?"

1 – A Brief Presentation of Catholic Schools

In his book on Catholic schools, Bishop Dominique Rey, bishop of Fréjus, informs us that "[private] Catholic schools include 20% of all students. They have two million children enrolled in them, even though this number masks a great diversity in their situations. More than one out of every two young people has spent at least one year of their lives as students in a Catholic establishment."[178]

In order to assess the value of the formation given in most official Catholic schools, it is important to know that ever since Vatican Council II (1962-1965), a new way of thinking has invaded the Church. The Church authorities have said it themselves. Cardinal Joseph Suenens, one of the liberal figures of the Council, asserted that "[Vatican Council II]

---

[178] Bishop Dominique Rey, *Urgence éducative*, Salvator, 2010, p. 8.

was 1789 in the Church."[179] Fr. Yves Congar, an expert at the Council and a future cardinal, presented Vatican Council II as "the October Revolution in the Church," in an allusion to the Russian revolution of 1917. Cardinal Ratzinger himself wrote of the document *Gaudium et Spes* on the Church's relations with the world, "Let us simply remark that the text serves as a counter-Syllabus[180] and, as such, represents, on the part of the Church, an attempt at an official reconciliation with the new era inaugurated in 1789."[181] Commenting on this pastoral constitution, Fr. Laurentin wrote that "a preferential consideration of the positive side is substituted for a unilateral consideration of the negative side. (…) This humble and positive consideration of the world is the preliminary condition for dialogue."[182]

This reconciliation between the Church and the world has had repercussions on the field of education. The desire to be up-to-date has progressively created a distance from the traditional form of education. That is why these institutions, even if some avoid the extreme deviations of many secular schools, today follow a way of thinking that is deeply out of keeping with the spirit transmitted to Catholics by the popes up until Vatican Council II.

In his book *Urgence éducative*, Bishop Rey states:

> Catholic schools fulfill a social function. [They] accomplish this service along with other public establishments and educational bodies, in a climate of dialogue and respect. Catholic schools thus ensure by their presence educational and religious pluralism[183] and, above all, the freedom and right each family has to choose their children's education. Lastly, by this openness to all, Catholic school allows for a real encounter and confrontation between cultures and religions, not only among young people but also among adults (teachers and other staff members) with very different histories.[184]

---

179 Quoted by Archbishop Marcel Lefebvre, *Sermon*, Ecône, Aug. 22, 1976.

180 The *Syllabus* is a Roman document by Pope Pius IX at the end of the 19th century condemning the principal modern errors.

181 Cardinal Ratzinger, *Principles of Catholic Theology*, Ignatius Press, 1987.

182 Fr. Laurentin, *Bilan du concile Vatican II*, Seuil, 1967, p. 182-183.

183 "Less than 12% of French families consider a Christian education as their first reason for choosing to enroll their children in a Catholic school." Bishop Dominique Rey, *Urgence* éducative, Salvator, 2010, p. 139.

184 Bishop Dominique Rey, *Urgence éducative*, Salvator, 2010, p. 143.

In fact, opening Catholic schools to children and adults of every human and spiritual horizon out of an excessive fear of isolationism and elitism can only lead the children formed in these schools to indifferentism and relativism.

What is more, besides the fact that children from every possible background attend these so-called Catholic schools, it is also important to know that today these schools are obliged to apply strictly all the State school programs, with everything that implies for the intellectual and moral formation of children, as we are now going to consider.

As Bishop Cattenoz, bishop of Avignon, admitted in September 2006, "many Catholic establishments have nothing Catholic left about them except their name."[185]

2 – A New Way of Teaching

Before we take a look at the school programs in public schools and the official Catholic schools, here are a few considerations on the teaching methods prescribed in these establishments.

Bishop Rey tells us that "over 35% of young Frenchmen have a hard time reading at the age of 18! 100,000 young Frenchmen out of 800,000 can barely read or cannot read at all at the end of their obligatory school years! 80% of the students who fail to learn to read in 1st grade never make up the lost time. These numbers accuse the renewal of teaching methods in the 1970s, that insisted on the global method (or mixed method) for learning the language, on spontaneity, creativity… to the detriment of memorization and the structured acquisition of fundamental notions (math, spelling, recitation…)."[186]

Jean Sévillia, in his book entitled *Moralement correct*, corroborates this analysis:

> A dictation given by the group *Sauvez les lettres* shows that, based on the 1970 correction criteria, 56% of high schoolers in 2004 would score a 0.[187]

Today, these new methods for learning the language and the invasion of images through the media have progressively led to the destruction of the intelligence. As the philosopher Jean-Jacques Wunenberger recalls,

---

185 Quoted by Jean Sévillia, *Moralement correct*, Perrin, 2008, p. 39.

186 Bishop Dominique Rey, *Urgence éducative*, Salvator, 2010, p. 17.

187 Jean Sévillia, *Moralement correct*, Perrin, 2008, p. 28.

"the food of images captures the attention and stuns the conscience, inhibiting the superior functions of the mind."[188]

And as authority is considered an obstacle to freedom, it tends to disappear little by little. "The superiority of the educator over the educated is less and less compatible with the regime of equality," remarks Alain Renaut.[189]

Marie Giral declares that nowadays "the rules are negotiated, they have to be consensual, under the pain, for those who decree them, of seeming fascist or reactionary."[190] They, therefore, seek to establish a consensus between parents, children, and professors, the fruit of a mythical equality.

As Jean Sévillia points out, "in university institutions for the formation of teachers, teachers are explicitly invited to refrain from discipline, on the pretext that the sanction could be 'misunderstood.' They are advised 'not to punish the students' but to 'speak with them,' in order to 'build a democratic authority.'"[191]

Pascal Bruckner declares, "Learning is assimilated to a persecution; the objective is to help students blossom, not to inflict abstract knowledge upon them."[192]

A professor in a mixed-sex Catholic middle school mostly attended by middle-class children, responded as follows to the question, "What about the teaching methods themselves?":

> The goal of teaching is no longer to teach but to make the students discover. We are not allowed to impose knowledge, for that supposes a form of psychological constraint and causes the child to reject it, and all of this is considered by the inspectors as unacceptable and punished as such. At least that is the way it is here. (...) Hence the advantage of teaching histories and educational projects that are a sort of practical study. Generally speaking, we are not supposed to impose knowledge and say that 2 plus 2 is 4.[193]

---

188 Quoted by André Bergevin, *Révolution permissive*, François-Xavier de Guibert, 2003, p. 331.

189 Alain Renaut, *La Fin de l'autorité*, Flammarion, 2004, p. 149.

190 Marie Giral, *Les Adulescents*, Le Pré aux Clercs, 2002, p. 141.

191 Report on an *IUFM* in the Val-de-Marne (*Le Figaro*, Feb. 1, 2006), cited and commented on by Jean Sévillia in *Moralement correct*, Perrin, 2008, p. 25.

192 Pascal Bruckner, *L'Euphorie perpétuelle*, Grasset, 2000.

193 Monique Lefevre, *Cahiers Saint-Raphaël* n. 83, *Quelle jeunesse pour demain?*, June 2006, p. 49.

They ask the child's opinion as if he were an adult. They come to terms on a contract, a work and discipline agreement. The student builds up his knowledge and establishes his own personal project. "The constitutive values of modernity entail the contractualization of the relations between persons."[194] Several schools in France, both private and public, thus strive to make teaching methods *evolve*.

Christine Legrand tells us that "the *Louez-Dieu* middle school in Arras has created 'project classes.' The students choose their classes based on a dominant subject (theater, sports, science, communication, art); they can cultivate their garden or create television reports."[195]

As far as the authority of the teachers goes, Bishop Rey explains that:

> . . . the teacher's authority is disputed by the parents themselves, as are the measures he should take. Parents tend to defend their child more and more. Teachers constantly have to justify what they are teaching and their reasons for teaching it. They have to teach, enforce discipline, and constantly negotiate with the parents and children, all at the same time.[196]

"Indeed," laments Marie Giral, "many parents systematically side with their child; 'You are right, that teacher is awful. I'll go talk to him if he keeps bothering you.'"[197]

Many see authority as an obstacle to freedom. So they replace it with a sort of contract in which one obeys the law one has set for oneself. The natural relation is replaced by a contractual relation. Already in control of the political power, Rousseau triumphs in the family and at school. This new teaching method, taken to an extreme, leads to absolute individualism.

Pope Pius XI, who saw a new conception of man and freedom spreading, condemned

> those modern systems bearing various names which appeal to a pretended self-government and unrestrained freedom on the part of the child, and which diminish or even suppress the teacher's authority and action, attributing to the child an exclusive primacy of initiative, and an activity independent of any higher law, natural or divine, in the work of his education. [The modern philosophers and educators imbued with these

---

194 Alain Renaut, *La Fin de l'autorité*, Flammarion, 2004, p. 133.

195 Christine Legrand, "Inventons le collège de demain," *La Croix*, Apr. 6, 2011, p. 13-14.

196 Bishop Dominique Rey, *Urgence éducative*, Salvator, 2010, p. 78.

197 Marie Giral, *Les Adulescents*, Le Pré aux Clercs, 2002, p. 258.

> systems] are miserably deluded in their claim to emancipate, as they say, the child, while in reality they are making him the slave of his own blind pride and of his disorderly affections, which, as a logical consequence of this false system, come to be justified as legitimate demands of a so-called autonomous nature.[198]

3 – History and Geography Programs

A quick glance at the history and geography programs will show how the State wishes to determine man's conduct in the 21st century.

In history class, students no longer study events chronologically, but rather thematically. A public-school history teacher, who prefers to remain anonymous, explains:

> For the past several years, the history programs no longer follow a chronological order, but simply cover distinct periods. Four levels (the sixth, seventh, eighth, and tenth grades) cover twenty-four centuries of history, and the other three (the ninth, eleventh, and twelfth grades) study the last two centuries of our history.
>
> What is more, history is presented in themes: "the Athenian democracy" and "the Mediterranean in the 12th century," to illustrate cultural tolerance; "the Renaissance," the period when men began to think and create again; "the Enlightenment," when men spoke of Equality and Freedom. And above all, one must not forget Jules Ferry, the inventor of obligatory, free, and secular schools.
>
> The fact this reform was conducted in a climate of intolerance and to the exclusion of religious congregations is of no importance; the facts are covered up. It is impossible to question the official version and say that the Republican left-wing acts intolerantly. Who can contradict this version that has been *sealed* for more than a century?
>
> The historical truth would demand that we say that free schools had existed in convents and parishes ever since the Middle Ages, and that an edict from Louis XIV tried to make school obligatory in 1695 but was not fully applied. Jules Ferry may have reinvented these two aspects, but he is certainly the inventor of lay secularism: that has never been neutral! This is only one out of hundreds of examples.
>
> In the current history program, the emphasis is placed on the knowledge of the present, in the interest of inculcating a specific ethical and political behavior.

---

[198] Pius XI, *Divini Illius Magistri*, Dec. 31, 1929.

> Pierre Lunel explains that the sickness has a name: *presentism*. History, in our days, is that which is happening today, history class is a form of journalism. The only historical depth is that which comes from myself.[199]

The history professor goes on to say:

> In the school system, history is not a knowledge of the past to cultivate oneself, take a step back and understand man; it is a *catechism*. The purpose of history programs is to make students assimilate simple concepts: democracy, equality, tolerance, human dignity. Ever since the Third Republic, history has been instrumentalized, and many 20th-century totalitarian regimes have done the same in order to form minds docile to their ideologies. Only the interesting periods that illustrate the ideas to be inculcated into minds are studied.

As Fr. Bourrat, director of the education in the Society of Saint Pius X schools in France since 2011, wrote:

> With this method, the State and the world powers that require States to implement this indoctrination seek to eradicate any trace of Christian civilization, voluntarily deforming and denying the Church's role in history, her work of education, civilization, culture, moralization, her works of charity that provided support for the poorest and most unhealthy, her entire doctrine that leads men to Heaven and not to the illusion of a simply earthly life. History is a connection with our cultural and religious roots. It should be a source of culture and of a critical mind, of moral judgment, too, capable of arming the mind against the disciples of a totalitarianism that hides its true name. The particularity of totalitarianism has always been to insinuate itself into minds, demanding submission to a State power in charge of regulating everything, even minds and religion.[200]

In geography class, the official program includes the question of sustainable development. This is the recurring theme studied in the seventh and tenth grades. Without going so far as to judge the subject in itself, it is important to know that taken to its ultimate consequences, it includes Malthusian and alarming measures.

In the tenth grade, there is talk of "new needs for more than 9 billion men in 2050" and consequently the need to "implement methods of sus-

---

199 Pierre Lunel, *La Manufacture des ânes*, L'Archipel, 2010, p. 49.

200 Fr. Philippe Bourrat, *Petite analyse des programmes de l'Education nationale de la sixième à la première*, Feb. 2011. Cf. Xavier Martin, *La France abîmée*, Dominique Martin Morin, 2009, as well as his other works.

tainable development." Certain politicians propose, among other methods, to cease encouraging demographical growth in industrialized countries.[201] Political scientist Susan George, president of the *Observatory on Globalization*, speaks of reducing the world's population by two billion.

The paradise sought by the idolaters of the school system thus turns into a nightmare. A parallel can be made with the Sexual Revolution. It, too, promised happiness, but in return, it leads to the daily massacre of an incalculable number of innocents.

In speaking of the overpopulation of the earth, Pope Pius XII responded, "Providence reserves the world's future for itself. (...) God will not ask men to account for the general destiny of humanity, which is in His hands, but for the individual acts they themselves willed either in keeping with or in opposition to the precepts of the conscience."[202]

The pope drew the following conclusions:

> Overpopulation, therefore, is not a valid reason for diffusing illicit methods of birth control, but rather a pretext for legitimizing the avarice and selfishness either of nations that fear the growth of other nations as a danger for their own political hegemony and a risk of lowering their standard of living, or of individuals, especially the most comfortable, who prefer the most unlimited enjoyment of earthly goods to the honor and merit of raising up new lives. Thus do men end up violating certain laws of the Creator under the pretext of correcting the imaginary mistakes of Providence.[203]

Because human beings are endowed with intelligence, it is important to reflect upon the means for developing our countries' resources and for distributing them better. Monsignor Schooyans, a member of the *Pontifical Council for the Family* and a counselor for the *Pontifical Academy for Life*, says that it is important to avoid simplistic arguments that associate a large population with poverty. Singapore is a counterexample of this, as are the Netherlands and Belgium. They are wealthy countries even though they have a dense population, thanks to their ingenuity, creativity, and the way they work, and the structure of their organization. There

---

[201] For example, Antoine Waecher, regional counselor of Alsace in 2010, quoted by Eric Letty, "Se passer du nucléaire et réduire la démographie," *Monde et vie*, no. 841, April 2011, p. 10.

[202] Pius XII, *Speech to the Council of the Italian Federation of the Association of Large Families*, Jan. 20, 1958.

[203] *Ibidem.*

are countries where the social organization is such that all its members are better off contributing to the common good.

Msgr. Schooyans also denounces a certain number of social structures, such as Islam, in which men are not encouraged to wake up. He also decries the fact that, in a certain number of African societies, individual initiatives are made impossible because as soon as someone creates wealth, it is immediately seized by his cousins, in-laws, *etc.* It is not for nothing that the Western countries are the most developed.[204]

4 – Permissive Teaching Methods

Public and subsidized private schools are not content with conditioning minds to adapt them to a globalized economy and a pluralist society marked by a new religiosity. They also promote a moral conduct in keeping with their conception of man and life.

A New Conception of Man

In public schools, man is made sacred, endowed with divine prerogatives. Each individual is considered capable of founding his own morality, his own way of living. And paradoxically, while claiming to possess these prerogatives, he is debased to the level of an animal scarcely more developed than other animals.

The theory of evolution is taught as a dogma in elementary school. The National Education bulletin says that "in elementary school the students have been prepared for the theory of evolution."[205]

Here is an extract of the knowledge that is to be acquired on this subject in the ninth grade:

> The comparison of species leads one to suppose a relationship between them, which is explained by evolution. The cell, the smallest unit of living beings, and the universality of the substrate of the genetic information in all organisms including Man clearly indicate a common primordial origin. Man as a species appeared on Earth as part of the process of evolution.[206]

---

204 Extract from the conference *Le Nouvel ordre moral* by Anne-Marie Libert, given at the Université d'été de la Renaissance catholique, summer 2011.

205 *Bulletin officiel de l'Education nationale*, no. 32, Aug. 28, 2008.

206 *Ibidem.*

In the revolutionary conception of man, a new step has just been taken with gender theory, inserted into the science programs since the 2011 school year, in the eleventh grade. The Ministry of Education included it in the section "Feminine/Masculine" in new chapters on "Becoming a Man or Woman" and "Living Your Sexuality," that come after the section on "Mastering Procreation."[207]

This theory comes from feminist and homosexual circles. In the wake of Sartre's existentialism, gender theory opposes a biological sex of absolutely no value to a cultural, polymorphous gender, invented to suit sexual desires. In other words, one is not born a man or a woman; one is free to choose one's sexual orientation. Sexual identity is thus erased to leave only a freely chosen sexual orientation.

And this choice can only be made by each person intimately and privately and therefore it must be respected no matter what, under pain of discrimination, says François de Muizon:

> The ultimate objective is capital: the purpose is clearly to do away with sexual differences, with sex as a difference, as a limit that makes a relation of otherness possible, and thus to do away with the family.[208]

Alain Toulza points out the profoundly subversive nature of the gender theory and its consequences on the family:

> The fairly recent promotion of homosexuality crowns this undertaking to demolish all the barriers of sexuality and thus of the institution of the family. (…) The program of communitarian homosexual subversion is not limited, like atheistic materialism, to trying to oppose the sons of Adam to their God; it goes farther, and seeks more profoundly to modify the order of creation, to destroy human nature in its original duality and to reconstruct a sexually undifferentiated human creature (*gender*) whose species can be perpetuated thanks to the progress in biotechnology (beginning with medically assisted procreation[209]).[210]

---

[207] *Bulletin officiel de l'Education nationale*, no. 9, Sept. 30, 2010.

[208] François de Muizon, *Homme et femme, l'altérité fondatrice*, Cerf, 2008, p. 51.

[209] "In the case of medically assisted procreation with a third-party donor, no filiation can be established between the donor and the child born of this procreation." Law of July 29, 1994, article 311-19.

[210] Alain Toulza, *Cahiers Saint-Raphaël*, n. 89, *Quelle Société pour demain ?*, Dec. 2007, p. 45-46.

Paul-François Paoli remarks that "the complete being that unites in itself the quintessence of both sexes is the figment of a phantasm that denies sexual division and claims to precede this distinction. It fills our post-modern times that claim the individual chooses and builds himself."[211]

This claim, he concludes, "is the sign of a profound absence of existential humility and possibly of an anthropological degeneracy."[212]

Laxism and Catholic Liberalism

Immorality is now more than suggested in these schools; it is taught, sometimes insidiously, but surely. Sexual education began to spread in schools in the 1970's and has never ceased to evolve since, recalls Dr. Luc Perrel:

> Joseph Fontanet, mysteriously assassinated in Paris in February 1980, was the Minister of National Education under Giscard d'Estaing and imposed sexual education in the ninth grade. The AIDS affair served as a pretext to make condoms normal by presenting them as the absolute weapon against the disease, which is false. At present, they begin training children to handle the latex in kindergarten.[213]

In literary, linguistic, or scientific studies, everything serves as a pretext to excite unhealthy ideas in children and give them a licentious conception of life.

For example, ever since 2008, high schoolers are asked to study "erotic poetry" in Greek literature.[214] Latin scholars have to study the theme "desire and seduction."[215] If they specialize in Latin, they only have to study the complete work by Ovid entitled *The Art of Love*.[216] This work may not be pornographic strictly speaking, but it is gravely immoral. Many protests were heard when this program was published, but the minister did not see fit to change the book to be studied.

Literature students are obliged to study four complete works in the twelfth grade. It is rare for at least one of the four not to be gravely

---

211 Paul-François Paoli, *La Tyrannie de la faiblesse*, François Bourin, 2010, p. 195.

212 *Ibidem.*

213 Luc Perrel, *Cahiers Saint-Raphaël*, no. 76, *La France se meurt*, Sept. 2004, p. 97.

214 *Bulletin officiel de l'Education nationale*, no. 32, Sept. 13, 2007.

215 *Ibidem.*

216 June 2010 and June 2011 sessions.

immoral and an encouragement to debauchery and irreligion. For example, *Le Supplément au voyage de Bougainville* by Diderot, *Jacques le fataliste* by Diderot for the 2007 and 2008 sessions, *Les Liaisons dangereuses* by Choderlos de Laclos for the 2009 and 2010 sessions. And as if the text were not bad enough, students often have to study the movie based on the book as well.

"The fundamental notions of the transmission of life among human beings are taught in elementary school."[217] Besides these delicate elements, here is what an eighth grader is supposed to know:

> In the context of controlling reproduction, contraceptive methods make it possible to choose when or not to have a child. Contraception is the name for methods used to avoid a pregnancy reversibly and temporarily. Contraception can be chemical or mechanical.
>
> The specific way each form of contraception works will be learned the following year, in the ninth grade. [218]

Needless to say, the photos and drawings that illustrate these chapters in textbooks are rarely an incitement to the virtue of purity...

Pius XI saw this coming and warned parents against sexual education:

> Far too common is the error of those who with dangerous assurance and under an ugly term propagate a so-called sex-education. (...) Such persons grievously err in refusing to recognize the inborn weakness of human nature (...) and also in ignoring the experience of facts, from which it is clear that, particularly in young people, evil practices are the effect not so much of ignorance of intellect as of weakness of a will exposed to dangerous occasions, and unsupported by the means of grace.[219]

Pope John Paul II also denounced the mistaken information given to young people regarding the transmission of life:

> The Church is firmly opposed to an often widespread form of imparting sex information dissociated from moral principles. That would merely be an introduction to the experience of pleasure and a stimulus leading to the loss of serenity—while still in the years of innocence—by opening the way to vice.[220]

---

217 *Bulletin officiel de l'Education nationale*, no. 32, Sept. 13, 2007.

218 *Ibidem.*

219 Pius XI, *Divini Illius Magistri*, Dec. 31, 1929.

220 John Paul II, Apostolic Exhortation *Familiaris Consortio*, Nov. 22, 1981, §37.

Teaching immorality in schools comes along with practice, made all the easier by the introduction of co-education.

In officially Catholic schools, they doubtless do not go so far as to claim that man depends only on himself and that he can act however he wishes, but the current religious authorities no longer see the world and the enemies of the Church the same way their predecessors did. Many Churchmen since Vatican Council II no longer see the intrinsic malice of the Freemasonic ideology. They prefer to see the world in a positive light and to dialogue with it. They thus encourage children to try to get along with everyone in their school, in a harmony based on respect for the opinions of others, listening, sharing, and avoiding any proselytism that is considered incompatible with religious freedom.

Bishop Rey describes his own attitude towards the world in the following terms:

> Paradoxically, whereas Christianity has been suspected of obscurantism ever since the Enlightenment, one of the major contributions of the Church today could be that of believing in reason, in the intelligence of our world, and in reminding our society of the desire for truth buried in it, accompanying it in its quest, all the while having not only the courage to proclaim her convictions but also the humility to accept to be instructed.[221]

Churchmen today, in the spirit of Vatican II, thus seem to believe in the intelligence of the atheistic and perverse world, to the point of asking Catholics to have the humility to learn from it. It seems to us that this new attitude, far from contributing to the reestablishment of the reign of Our Lord Jesus Christ on earth, only contributes to a greater spread of the Revolution, which has already reached a frightful degree of perversity.

Fr. Roussel's judgment in 1926 is truer than ever today:

> The liberal Catholic, whose intention was to reconcile the Church with the Revolution, actually allowed, made possible, and facilitated the conquests of the Revolution; he won nothing on the left, lost much on the right, made no conversions, contributed to many perversions and apostasies.[222]

---

[221] Bishop Dominique Rey, *Urgence éducative*, Salvator, 2010, p. 36-37.

[222] A. Roussel, *Libéralisme et catholicisme*, reports presented at the *Semaine Catholique* in 1926, p. 80-81.

5 – Conclusion

Ever since the 1990's, European education programs have entered into a new phase of man's formation. The ideology imposed everywhere in schools has already borne bitter fruit in the social realm. The decadence has been all the speedier since there was practically no resistance from the clergy. Things have gone from tolerance to transgression, inspiring this cry of alarm from François de Muizon:

> In a society that tends to be individualistic and narcissist, the new subjective norms are easily imposed. All the recent homosexual demands (gay marriage, adoption, laws on homophobia) impose this radical change of mentality, under the cover of good sentiments and behind the mask of the very respectable fight against discrimination. (…) There is an urgent need to understand the foundations of this new ideology, which is welcomed on a massive scale today with the same naïve blindness with which the great ideologies of the 20th century were welcomed in their day.[223]

We deplore the fact that many parents unfortunately do not realize the harm done by the current education system. Often it is only once they no longer have any control over the situation, when their children reach adolescence, that they begin to react. They are surprised to see their children abandon the principles they wished to pass on to them, for they do not realize that the cause is the type of education they were given.

---

[223] François de Muizon, *Homme et femme, l'altérité fondatrice*, Cerf, 2008, p. 51.

CHAPTER TWENTY-SIX

What School for Our Children?

Seeing the teaching and formation given in secular and so-called Catholic schools, parents spontaneously wonder, "Where can we enroll our children? Is there any way to escape the dictatorship of the modern way of thinking?"

1 – The Choice of a Truly Catholic School

The bishops of France of the past century never ceased to exhort families to place their children in a truly Catholic establishment. We saw at the beginning of this chapter what this name "Catholic" implies.

Here are examples from two bishops of France in 1936 and 1954:

> It goes without saying that parents will choose a Christian school for their son if there is one at their disposal. We just said that in order to develop, a vocation needs a favorable atmosphere. And it is clear that neutral schools are not a favorable atmosphere for them, since they are legally obliged to profess secularism, that is to say that they are not allowed to speak of God, that they lock the child's mind up in the exclusive knowledge of the things of the present life, and give morality a purely human foundation.[224]

> The most effective contribution on the part of Catholic families will clearly consist in choosing Christian schools for their children, which only supposes the simple fulfillment of an essential obligation. The doctrine of the Church is clear on this point.[225]

Pope Pius XII gave parents the following directives to help them choose a good school for their children:

---

[224] Archbishop Louis Marmottin, Archbishop of Reims, *Lettre pastorale*, 1954.

[225] Bishop Jean-Baptiste Mégnin, bishop of Angoulême, *Lettre pastorale*, 1936.

> Oppose the pernicious efforts to completely remove religion from education and schools, or at least to found schools and education on a purely naturalistic basis, with the ideal of a teaching rich in the inestimable treasure of a sincere faith vivified by the grace of Our Lord Jesus Christ.[226]

From 1970 to 1975, certain Catholic parents, who had received the special grace of realizing the disaster that was going to come of the new orientations chosen by the so-called Catholic schools, understood that they could not leave their children in those schools without danger. But where to send them?

Pope Pius XII once declared, "The Church will fight to the end for Catholic schools and the Catholic formation of teachers, in order to ensure the existence and well-being of Catholic families and their children."[227]

Animated by this spirit, teaching Sisters, seeing the decadence of the official Catholic schools, preferred to leave their congregation in order to found their own establishments rather than follow this new orientation. In other places, parents also came together to found fully Catholic schools and some turned to institutions such as the Priestly Society of Saint Pius X to run these schools.

In these establishments, religion is not presented as an ordinary subject taught a few hours a week. It permeates the entire formation. From morning prayers to evening prayers, the child bathes in a profoundly Catholic atmosphere. The real presence of Jesus in the Eucharist in the middle of the school reminds him of the necessity of living in His presence and in dependency on Him. The efforts he makes during class and study hall are also stimulated by the sweet presence of the Divine Master, under the protection of His Holy Mother. The community life, too, becomes peaceful and joyful when each member of the school does his bit.

Fr. Calmel gave the following description of the atmosphere that reigns in the schools of the Dominicans of the Holy Name of Jesus:

> The school climate of our houses is a climate of honesty, joy, and trust. Far from implying anarchy and lack of discipline, this supposes a prelimi-

---

226 Pius XII, *Speech to the Members of the International Institute of Public Finances*? Oct. 2, 1948.

227 Pius XII, *Speech to a group of Catholic teachers from Bavaria*, Dec. 31, 1956.

> nary agreement that is recognized and accepted. It is an agreement on four main points: docility and discipline, poverty, purity, and Faith.[228]

2 – Answers to Some Objections

Giving one's children a Catholic education requires very great sacrifices on the financial level. Some parents hesitate to make this choice.

Here is what Bishop Mégnin had to say:

> Financial considerations sometimes turn families away from Christian schools. (…) We agree that this excuse can cause some hesitation. However, it is not peremptory. (…) We boldly declare that even if this sacrifice is inconvenient, so long as it is possible, Christian parents must accept it. Let them judge with their faith and they will agree. The education of their children will not appear to them as some luxurious expense that can be eliminated with the others from a tightening budget. In truth, it takes the first rank among the necessary expenses.[229]

On top of the financial sacrifices, there is the geographical distance which presents yet another obstacle for parents. Some sidestep this difficulty by moving closer to truly Catholic schools. But this solution is not always possible, and a number of parents hesitate to let their children leave home for boarding school.

Boarding school certainly does not present only benefits, but nor does it present only drawbacks. Boarding students can be divided into three categories.

There are those who ask their parents of their own accord to send them to boarding school, sometimes to their great surprise. Some of them already hear the call of a religious or priestly vocation and realize that it will only blossom in this sort of setting. Doubtless, these are exceptions, but they are not as rare as all that.

In the vast majority of cases, children are placed in boarding school without being asked for their opinion. Many children adjust easily. They find their balance under the double and complementary influence of the family and the school.

---

228 Fr. Calmel, *Ecole chrétienne renouvelée*, Téqui, 1990, p. 159.

229 Bishop Jean-Baptiste Mégnin, bishop of Angoulême, *Lettre pastorale*, 1936.

Lastly, there is a third category, children who for the moment undergo boarding school more than they accept it. But with time, some of them change their opinion on this form of life.

Here is what Fr. Laurençon, a priest of the Society of Saint Pius X, with his experience after eighteen years as director of the school of Saint-Michel in Châteauroux, has to say:

> In this latter category, there are children who remain victims for the entire time they are in school of a radical allergy to and an insurmountable repugnance for boarding life. One can imagine the martyrdom of parents who see their child filled with a destructive resentment and feel themselves accused of not seeking a solution better adapted to his desires. Only time and life experience can put an end to such a mental block, as the yearly alumni reunions go to show.
>
> Indeed, some of the most assiduous at these reunions are rebellious characters who, after having fled boarding school to the point of being expelled, come back as its best apostles. With their own experience, they know how to convince the younger children that this austere life also has its benefits. Thanks to the discipline and the community spirit acquired in these conditions, they were more capable than others of taking on responsibilities in the world, due to their ability to react to difficulties and adapt to all sorts of new situations."
>
> A mother whose seven sons went to boarding school corroborates this testimony: Boarding school forges stronger characters; community life is a good training for life. Besides, it favors strong friendships that are a help for life as a college student.[230]

A young seminarian assessed his years as a boarder in the Society of Saint Pius X schools in the following terms:

> These school years were a great grace for me. The most striking memory I have is the frequent reception of the sacraments and even more the closeness with the priests; being able to benefit from their advice and help every day at any time was a special grace for me and I think that it was mostly thanks to this contact with them and seeing their availability for souls that I really thought several times of a priestly vocation, to which, with the grace of God, I wish to try to respond.
>
> Another good memory of these schools is the healthy atmosphere that reigned in them, both in class, where we did not have to constantly sort the false from the true, and among each other, with relations marked by

---

[230] Testimony of a mother whose children went to the school of Saint-Joseph-des-Carmes in Montréal-de-l'Aude (11).

> healthy fraternal charity. Even if there were quarrels and tensions sometimes, we lived in a climate of trust, and in, difficulties, we could count on our comrades.[231]

Even if boarding school is not the best-suited situation for educating all children, it is still true that in the majority of cases, life in a truly Catholic boarding school is less restrictive than some parents think. In general, it provides children with a perfectly satisfactory formation.

Another reason invoked by parents for not placing their children in these schools is the fear of making them incapable of living in today's world.

Fr. Calmel answered this objection in his book *Ecole chrétienne renouvelée*:

> Our society is not sufficiently Christian, and nor is our civilization. Everyone agrees on this. In a civilization that is such, it is not possible to try to give a Christian teaching without going against the grain and rowing against the current.
>
> It is important to form Christians who, without being ignorant of the current civilization, will try to set it right. They will be formed in the present civilization, for we do not live on Sirius, but for the elaboration of a fully Christian civilization.[232]

Fr. Bourrat explains in a letter for the *Association de Défense de l'Ecole Catholique* that

> Giving a child a Catholic school provides him, not with the tranquility of a cocoon that would keep him from knowing the reality of the world and adapting to it one day, but with the conditions for a lucid education that, taking into consideration nature and grace, gives him the arms of truth before sending him into the fight, and makes him know and love the God Who created and saved him before confronting him with the oppositions of the world. Traditional schools are not pink clouds floating above reality, they are the place where he is trained and formed for real life, with a pace and means adapted to the child's development. One does not send a soldier to war without a minimum of training beforehand. Ignoring the reality

---

231 Testimony of a student who attended the school of Saint-Jean Baptiste-de-la-Salle, in Camblain-l'Abbé (62).

232 Fr. Calmel, *Ecole chrétienne renouvelée*, Téqui, 1990, p. 30.

> of the contemporary moral and intellectual combat would be the mark of a guilty blindness. Hence the necessity of a suitable school formation.[233]

It is true that the children formed in truly Catholic establishments live mostly sheltered from the world, but this is not an obstacle to their future integration into this world. The formation received at school will enable them to escape the pitfalls they will encounter later on and will make them capable of living serenely, sufficiently armed to keep their virtue.

They will even be ready to work for the salvation of the world, as Pius XII pointed out:

> The students of a Catholic institution, he wrote, should never consider their future career as a simple social function, necessary for themselves and those around them but without any immediate relation to their condition as baptized souls. Let them always consider it as the exercise of a responsibility in the work of saving the world, by which, committing seriously as Christians on the temporal level, they fulfill their highest spiritual destiny.[234]

To make the best choice of school, nothing is more helpful than visiting a profoundly Catholic school.

To the extent that they seek the true good of their child, parents will then be the first to benefit from their sacrifices in the abundant fruits that will come of them, be they spiritual,[235] moral, or intellectual.

---

233 Fr. Philippe Bourrat, *Lettre de l'Association de Défense de l'Ecole Catholique*, no. 19, Sept. 2011, p. 2-3.

234 Pius XII, *Speech for the 3rd General Assembly of the International Office of Catholic Teaching*, Sept. 14, 1958.

235 For example, today in France, 80% of the priestly vocations in the Society of Saint Pius X are young men formed in these schools.

CHAPTER TWENTY-SEVEN

Collaboration between the Family and the School

Pope Pius XII said that "the collaboration between parents and teachers must be constant and profound."[236] Consequently, when parents choose a truly Catholic school, they have not yet fulfilled their mission. It is also necessary for them not to go against the education given in the school by a certain slackness at home, against which Fr. Charmot warns:

> With an interior and exterior discipline, [children] will strengthen the first salutary habits acquired in middle school. For if, when going from school to home, children also go from order to disorder, from recollection to dissipation, from exact obedience to vague insubordination, from regulated work to capricious laziness, from government of their senses to satisfying their appetites, from respect for authority to mocking criticism, from serious piety to a superficial and stylish Christianity and so on, it is obvious that nothing that is done is not undone at the same rate; in a word, no formation is possible.[237]

These remarks made in 1933 still apply today. However, alongside the weakness of certain families, the priests and other educators in traditional circles have the very great consolation of seeing so many parents who, besides the great financial and emotional sacrifices they accept in order to give their children an education in keeping with their religious convictions, truly strive to work hand in hand with the heads of the institutions in which they have enrolled their children. In these families, at home and at school, many children strive to put God in His proper

---

[236] Pius XII, *Speech to Italian High School Teachers*, Jan. 5, 1954.

[237] Fr. François Charmot, *Esquisse d'une pédagogie familiale*, Clovis, 2006, p. 25.

place in their life through daily prayer and frequent reception of the sacraments. They do their best to respect their dignity as children of God even in their way of dressing. At home and at school, they have a sense of and respect for authority, and they seek to accomplish their duty of state conscientiously. The parents are thus rewarded and savor the delicious fruits produced by a true harmony between the family and the school.

CHAPTER TWENTY-EIGHT

A Just Solution for Financing Schools

In paying their taxes, Catholics contribute to the budget of the National Education and partially to that of subsidized private schools. Consequently, when they place their children in a private school, they have to pay all over again to give them a truly Catholic education.

Archbishop Marmottin, after recalling the State's duty to the family, denounced this injustice just after World War II in one of his pastoral letters:

> Promoting the common good is the essential function of the State in every domain. Within the country, this common good is the peace and security of families and individuals in the exercise of their legitimate rights; it is also their material and spiritual progress, ensured by the coordination of the efforts of all. First and foremost, this demands that honest and virtuous, hard-working citizens, devoted to their fellow men, be formed by a good education. (...)
>
> The State, which is everyone's institution, which is not a private business with personal interests and specific clients, must make available the school [that parents] desire; it receives from them to this end the tax they pay like everyone else to contribute to the budget of the National Education. Would it not be unjust for it to use this tax for the construction and upkeep only of public schools? (...)
>
> Catholics are obliged to provide [the government] with these subsidies for schools they do not use, and at the same time, to pay all over again to found the schools and pay the teachers they desire. Is this just? We might add: is this in keeping with the democratic equality that is so strongly advocated in our country? A revolutionary writer said not so long ago, "The head of a family who, in the name of his right, chooses for his children a free school that respects the legal conditions cannot, as a citizen and taxpayer, be penalized and obliged to pay twice."

> Freedom is no longer respected by this injustice. It truly is not, for the lower classes, the poor who cannot pay double, do not have this freedom to choose, and suffer in their consciences for sending their children to public school.[238]

Still today, this injustice puts a heavy strain on the budget of Catholic families. Anne Coffinier, president of the *Fondation pour l'école*, estimates that a child enrolled in a non-subsidized school saves the State about $8,500 per year.[239] Given the high cost of non-subsidized schools, parents wonder how they are going to make ends meet.

A school coupon, that is to say, the equivalent of a vacation allowance, would certainly be the most just solution to resolve this difficulty. This proposition has the support of the public opinion, as can be seen from a survey conducted in June 2010. The results of this survey by the *IFOP/Fondation pour l'école* show that 74% of the participants want the State to implement a system to allow each family to finance their children's schooling no matter what establishment they choose. The school coupon would indeed be the most coherent system to allow for a just distribution of the budget destined for the youth.

Conclusion of the Article

Between 1880 and 1950, the pope and the bishops never ceased to warn Catholics against so-called neutral schools. Over and over again, they denounced in their writings the disastrous results for children. And these results were not long in making themselves felt. It is no exaggeration to say that these schools played an important role in the de-Christianization of our country.

Bishop Nègre said so very clearly:

> In the eyes of the sovereign pontiffs, nothing justifies public schools in which a positive law has officially forbidden any religious teaching. The cause they defend is great and sacred, it is the cause of the small and the weak, the cause of the children of whom Jesus Christ said, "Woe to those who scandalize them!" (Lk. 17:1-2). Terrible, too, is the evil from which the popes seek to preserve souls, the family, and society; it is the evil that

---

[238] Archbishop Louis Marmottin, Archbishop of Reims, *Lettre pastorale*, 1946.

[239] *Le Cri du contribuable*, Aug. 30, 2011.

> engenders all the others, the evil of atheism, that the Psalmist describes in these terms: "The fool hath said in his heart: There is no God" (Ps. 13:1). And this fool immediately gave in to all the extravagances of vice, fell into corruption and committed abominable acts. "They are become abominable in their ways" (Ps. 13:1). May the words of those whom Jesus Christ has given to the faithful and to the world as spiritual guides put an end to these disorders by bringing God back into schools He should never have left.[240]

The evil described in speaking of public schools has today spread to the official Catholic schools. Children need coherency in their life. It is therefore very likely that they will stray from the Catholic Church once their time in school is over if they receive in school a formation that goes entirely against Catholic thought and is even deeply contrary to natural laws. This is the origin of the apostasy and religious indifference of so many children. Parents, therefore, who wish their children to remain faithful to the magnificent Catholic ideal will easily understand this ardent exhortation from Bishop Pasquet:

> Instructed by the cruel experience the country already has of irreligion, you can imagine, [dear parents,] if the little Faith it still lives on were to be lacking in the youth, all the harm that would come of its disappearance. And placing the salvation of your sons and your own salvation above promises or threats, you will take the necessary means to ensure it, certain that you love your country as much as others and even serve it better.[241]

Convinced of the importance of good schools, Bishop Manier wrote in 1927:

> Our Christian schools are the last refuge of the Faith, of the virtue and honor of childhood; we have to maintain and defend them at all costs. The end of them would be a terrible blow to religion; it would be the agony of France.[242]

---

[240] Bishop Albert Nègre, bishop of Tulle, *Lettre pastorale*, 1909.

[241] Bishop Octave Pasquet, bishop of Séez, *Lettre pastorale*, 1928.

[242] Bishop Adolphe Manier, bishop of Belley, *Lettre pastorale*, 1927.

ARTICLE IV

The Art of Being Grandparents

The role of educator principally goes to parents, but many other people can have a decisive influence on children's future. Grandparents sometimes play an essential role in the lives of one or another of their grandchildren.

> According to a study by the *INSEE* published in May 2021, grandparents represent 20% of the population. For several years now, people have been becoming grandparents later, since children have children later, but with the increasing length of life, two million grandparents are also great-grandparents.[243]

Grandparents are a delicate subject to discuss. Indeed, young grandparents often wish to pass on a certain number of principles or rules of behavior to their grandchildren and believe they have certain rights over them. They hope perhaps that what they are about to read here will support their request and give them free rein to ensure this transmission in the best conditions.

But fathers and mothers, for their part, find that their own parents seek to have too much control over their children and hope the boundaries grandparents should not overstep will be clearly defined.

---

[243] Marie Giral, *Les Adulescents,* Le Pré aux Clercs, 2002, p. 262-263.

CHAPTER TWENTY-NINE

The Authority and Influence of Grandparents

How are we to reconcile the desire of grandparents, who tend to want an ever-greater influence over their grandchildren, with that of parents, who rather seek to limit this influence? A look at principles will resolve this difficulty.

In the realm of education, a principle very clearly defines the limits of each party's behavior. According to the natural order, the responsibility for the children's formation goes first of all to the parents. They turn to others to perfect their children's education, but it is still they who are responsible for it.

Consequently, grandparents have no direct authority or direct power over their grandchildren. This does not mean, however, that their role is insignificant or their influence nonexistent. While it is very limited in certain cases, there are other cases in which it is dominant.

It is true that nowadays, several factors limit grandparents' influence. The first is geographical distances. Back when the different generations lived side by side, grandparents had a much greater influence. The extremely fast evolution of the world also limits the influence of grandparents in certain cases and to a certain extent. This evolution makes the distance between generations much greater. The development of computers and the means of communication, as well as the religious and moral decadence, plunges children at a very young age into the virtual realm and into a world very different from the world their parents knew at the same age. As children are used to living in an entirely artificial world, their grandparents sometimes seem like dinosaurs to them.

But it would be a mistake to generalize. While grandparents do not always have the place they would like to have in the family, their influence over their grandchildren can nonetheless be very beneficial and sometimes even decisive for their future. But this is only possible insofar as they are available for their grandchildren.

Children appreciate visiting their grandparents because of their love for them and the time they devote to them. They also like to hear them tell stories of the past and are particularly open to their spirit of piety.

The benefits of exemplary grandparents for their grandchildren are also proven by the feeling of frustration children experience when their grandparents are indifferent or sometimes even unworthy. Their disenchantment upon discovering some of their failings goes to show the important role faithful grandparents can play.

In general, grandparents' influence is all the deeper if it is exercised in the right order, that is to say, not against the parents and without their knowledge, but at least with their tacit consent. As grandparents' authority over their grandchildren is not direct but delegated, it is greater if it is effective, that is to say communicated explicitly or at least implicitly. If the exercise of their authority is more put up with than desired by the parents, the results for the grandchildren will be very limited.

What is more, for the influence of grandparents to be effective, it is also important for parents to transmit to their children a respect for their elders. This respect is disappearing more and more. There is the loss of the sense of authority and also the evolution of technology. A grandson knows more about certain subjects than his grandfather, and this discredits the older generations. Hannah Arendt pointed out that "the crisis of authority is closely connected with the crisis of tradition."[244] To the extent that grandchildren consider their grandparents as old-fashioned, poorly adapted to the world, and lacking in a sense of today's realities, their influence will become nonexistent.

While it is important to recover a sense of authority, it is also just as important to restore respect for one's elders.

Pope John Paul II wrote, "There are cultures which manifest a unique veneration and great love for the elderly: far from being outcasts from the family or merely tolerated as a useless burden, they continue to be

---

[244] Hannah Arendt, *La Crise de la culture*, Gallimard, 1972.

present and to take an active and responsible part in family life, though having to respect the autonomy of the new family; above all they carry out the important mission of being a witness to the past and a source of wisdom for the young and for the future.

> Other cultures, however, especially in the wake of disordered industrial and urban development, have both in the past and in the present set the elderly aside in unacceptable ways. This causes acute suffering to them and spiritually impoverishes many families.[245]

Pope Benedict XVI also pointed out the urgent need to restore to grandparents the place they deserve in the family:

> In the face of the crisis of the family, might it not be possible to set out anew precisely from the presence and witness of these people—grandparents—whose values and projects are more resilient? Indeed, it is impossible to plan the future without referring to a past full of significant experiences and spiritual and moral reference points. Thinking of grandparents, of their testimony of love and fidelity to life, reminds us of the Biblical figures of Abraham and Sarah, of Elizabeth and Zechariah, of Joachim and Anne, as well as of the elderly Simeon and Anna and even Nicodemus: they all remind us that at every age the Lord asks each one for the contribution of his or her own talents.[246]

---

[245] John Paul II, Apostolic Exhortation *Familiaris Consortio*, Nov. 22, 1981, §27.

[246] Benedict XVI, *Address to Participants in the Plenary Assembly of the Pontifical Council for the Family*, April 5, 2008.

CHAPTER THIRTY

Grandparents' Role

What exactly is the role of a grandfather? In his book *L'Art de vieillir*, Fr. Brugerette writes that "an education by the grandfather should not replace the education by the father, it is true. But as it is beneficial for the former to accompany the latter, the child's formation would be incomplete if the lessons of his ancestors did not accompany the lessons of his parents." He goes on to say:

> The father, caught up in the duties of life, all too often sees only the difficulties of daily tasks. He seeks to give his child the exterior means for his destiny but lacks the leisure to garnish the interior of his soul.
>
> The grandfather has finished his days of struggle and already looks down on human battles from a distance and with indifference; he is closer to the moment when all struggles are forgotten and has the time to go down into his soul and to see into others' souls. And while he does not provide the child with the instruments for an earthly victory, he can at least teach him the eternal meaning of things.
>
> And the grandfather, during the half-century of his past as a man, has seen so many children around him! He saw them be born, grow, triumph or fail or die. He saw as a small and weak child the man who is now a father and is making his proud beginnings in fatherhood. And he has a better knowledge of young ones and of what to say to them to excite their laughter or dry their tears.
>
> The experience of old age brings him closer to every age. So many reasons to live and to live usefully for those who were disillusioned by the indifference and ingratitude of the world!
>
> Like the child, the old man is fragile, and he is sensitive like him. He resembles the child in his heart and in his body. Grandparents and grandchildren's thoughts communicate, their tenderness and emotions reach

> out to each other and understand each other. It is as if they completed each other.[247]

To facilitate relations with their own children, grandparents should be especially tactful and delicate when the entire family is reunited. Indeed, it is important to distinguish between grandparents' role in the presence of the parents and the role they can have in their absence.

In the presence of the parents, grandparents should know how to remain discreet in their remarks to their grandchildren, so as not to offend the parents or undermine their authority. They should not take their place. It is important to enlighten, to pacify, to support everything good the parents transmit, a delicate exercise, Fr. Boubée explains:

> High aerobatics for grandparents: they are asked to remain silent, and yet to act. To see nothing, complain about nothing, and at the same time to correct, perfect, and complete everything. Parents themselves do not want the previous generation to be too intrusive.[248]

Grandparents have a greater authority over their grandchildren in the absence of the parents than in their presence. Indeed, grandparents are in charge in their own homes, and their grandchildren have to accept the rules of the house. But grandparents should always act as much as possible in the same way as the parents so that the children can keep the same references. And since their influence over their grandchildren is greater in the parents' absence, there is a quality that it is good for them to develop so that they can receive them in their own home: availability.

How should grandparents react when their own children seem to act mistakenly in the education of their grandchildren? It can be good for them to speak with them of the problematic issues, with the understanding that after they have spoken, it is up to the parents to shoulder their responsibilities.

If grandchildren are brought up poorly, how can they make up for what is lacking? Since the parents are the primary educators, the grandparents' influence will certainly be very limited if it goes against the influence of the parents and if their advice is not heeded. The situation is made all the more delicate by the fact that it is sometimes necessary to

---

247 Fr. Brugerette, *L'Art de vieillir*, Imprimerie de l'Est, 1926.

248 Fr. Jean-Pierre Boubée, *Le Chardonnet*, no. 255, Feb. 2010, p. 9.

overcome some particular difficulty regarding religious practice or the type of education given.

When grandparents' words are of no avail, they can still resort to prayer and example. When a direct intervention is too delicate, the communion of saints can still do much. Grandparents have saved couples on the point of separating with their prayers and sacrifices.

CHAPTER THIRTY-ONE

The Influence of Grandparents

The extent of a man's influence depends more on what he is than on what he says. Parents need to know this, but so do grandparents. It is therefore above all by their Christian virtues that they should shine.

First of all, grandparents should offer their grandchildren the beautiful example of conjugal fidelity. In this world where so many are unfaithful to their commitments, the example of fidelity is an encouragement for grandchildren. A pilgrimage chaplain once met two spouses in their sixties who showed such delicacy towards each other that it was both striking and touching. One would have thought they were on their honeymoon! They were a living model of fidelity in conjugal love after more than thirty years together, and all of the pilgrims were particularly edified. What a beautiful example! The importance of this conjugal fidelity is also proven by the scandal for grandchildren when their grandparents go astray.

A beautiful example of faith can also be extraordinarily effective. Here follows a few examples.

A very pious grandmother brought her granddaughter to Mass at Saint-Nicolas-du-Chardonnet from time to time. By helping her to follow the Mass, teaching her to pray, giving her the example of profound piety, she opened her mind and heart to spiritual realities. This was done discreetly but very effectively. Once married, this granddaughter chose the traditional Mass and brought her entire family to the Society of Saint Pius X.

Grandparents who had dreamed of having a son become a priest without seeing this dream fulfilled, nonetheless obtained this grace through one of their grandsons.

It is also important to take advantage of particular circumstances to show young people the right path. At his granddaughter's marriage, a grandfather was able to give her some guidelines with great delicacy and finesse.

There is also unfortunately the desolation of grandparents distressed at seeing that their children have not followed in their footsteps and their grandchildren are far from any religion.

In difficult situations, one must never despair. Take this example of a grandmother devastated that her two granddaughters had not been baptized. It was her greatest sorrow before her death. And on the day she was buried, her daughter decided to baptize her children. Grandparents' influence does not end with death.

Here is another example of the influence grandparents can have even after they have left this world. On March 8, 1919, a marriage was celebrated in the church of Chaudenay-la-Ville, a small parish in Burgundy. In his sermon, Fr. Félix Bertheau, the pastor, praised the two spouses. Here is an extract that gives an idea of the tone:

> I do not know, my dear children, what is the most admirable in your mutual friendship, the strength of this affection or the respect with which you love each other so tenderly. In all of my priestly life, I have never encountered so great an example of this first condition for marriage as in you.
>
> My dear friend, in the practice of every virtue, this dear child did not realize that for twenty-two years she was drawing down from the heart of God the graces that will make of her a generous wife, a tireless mother, the valiant woman of the testimony of the Holy Ghost.

Some time after the marriage, on June 1, the priest sent the young spouses a copy his sermon and wrote:

> You do not like praise, and I can only approve, but I add these lines so that your children and grandchildren, upon reading them, can see for their edification what their parents and grandparents were in their youth. Be assured, my dear children, of my affectionate and devoted sentiments.

Recently, one of their granddaughters found this text when she had just returned to religion and decided to regularize her matrimonial situation. These lines deeply moved her and made a strong impression. And this testimony written nearly a century ago greatly assisted her in making this step. Although her grandparents have been dead for a long time, this lady benefited from the example of their virtues. God sees farther than us!

Another attitude that is very edifying for those around them is the grandparents' serenity in the face of the progressive decline of their faculties. Elderly persons, by what they are, teach young people the vanity of earthly pleasures and the passing nature of earthly beauties. Simply by what they are, grandparents invite their grandchildren not to seek their happiness in everything that passes, but in that which is eternal. "For the fashion of this world passeth away," says St. Paul (I Cor. 7:31).

Conclusion of the Article

The interior man, instead of growing old, is renewed day after day. The secret to not growing old is to develop one's interior life. True youth is spiritual. That is the ultimate message grandparents should give their grandchildren to invite them to seek true joys where they are to be found, that is to say, in God, who is the owner of joy. An elderly person full of God is a living image of God Himself.

Here are a few words from Fr. Lacordaire to conclude this article:

> Hair whitened by the meditation of eternity, sacred colors of the soul that shine in old age and death, blessed are those who have seen you! More blessed still are those who have understood you and received your lessons of wisdom and immortality![249]

May all grandchildren have such examples before their eyes to follow upon the path of immortality!

[249] Fr. Henri-Dominique Lacordaire, "Le plan général de la création," *Conférences de Notre-Dame de Paris,* 48th conference, Lent 1848.

Conclusion of the Book

In the first section of this work, we saw that the profound changes affecting marriage that have taken place over the course of the past few decades are partially the result of laws that gravely attack marriage in its indissolubility and fertility.

This second section shows that the current upheavals that affect the family also come from attacks on the father, from separating children from their mother at a very young age, and from the type of education given in public schools and so-called Catholic schools.

For this reason, with their eyes open to the dangers presented by official institutions, certain parents choose to ensure the early education of their children themselves, by doing everything they can for the mother to stay home, and then entrust them to truly Catholic schools. They know that a Christian education is the fruit of a collaboration between priests, educators, parents, and even grandparents. They therefore do what they can so that everyone can work along the same lines to perfect this education. In this way, they are able to attenuate in their children the wounds left by original sin and to develop the virtues that will allow them to fully respond to God's demands as adults.

Bishop Pasquet, in one of his pastoral letters, quoted a book from the 1920's that studied the relations between Europe and America and wondered which of the two continents would one day come out on top. The author's answer was, "The people with the best school and the best family."

The bishop concluded:

> May these words be the Catholic byword in France! For in the conflict that has been going on for so long between the powers of evil and the powers of good, there are no more reassuring reserves today to make the

> powers of good triumph than the school and the family that have once again become completely Christian.[250]

What a joy to meet such families, whose parents are taken with this beautiful ideal, in which the husband and wife each fulfill their mission under God's eyes, in which the children are enrolled in truly Catholic schools!

In such a healthy and balanced atmosphere, it is naturally easier for children to obey. It is easy for them to grow accustomed to sacrifice and progressively form solid convictions.

Well brought-up, they will be capable tomorrow of transmitting to future generations the values they themselves have received. Indeed, in general, children who come from balanced families and have been formed in good schools blossom and are able to find their place in society and in the Church. They have solid convictions and walk serenely in this land of exile along the path to Heaven through the practice of Christian virtues.

One final word from Bishop Bernard:

> To work, then, [dear parents!] Look down on these young souls, radiant flowers entrusted to your care. Let them find in your faith and in your hearts the light, the warmth they need to blossom, remain fresh and sweet-smelling, and bear all the fruit God, the Church, and the country expect of them.[251]

---

[250] Bishop Octave Pasquet, bishop of Séez, *Lettre pastorale*, 1928.

[251] Bishop Henri Bernard, bishop of Perpignan, *Lettre pastorale*, 1942.